CREED
AND
CHRIST

A Devotional Approach to the Apostles' Creed

CREED AND CHRIST

RON JAMES

THE UPPER ROOM
Nashville, Tennessee

Scripture quotations not otherwise identified are from the Re-
vised Standard Version of the Bible, copyrighted 1946, 1952,
and © 1971 by the Division of Christian Education, National
Council of the Churches of Christ in the United States of
America, and are used by permission.

Scripture quotations designated AP are the author's paraphrase.

Scripture quotations designated NEB are from *The New English
Bible,* © The Delegates of the Oxford University Press and the
Syndics of the Cambridge University Press 1961 and 1970,
and are used by permission.

Scripture quotations designated KJV are from the King James
Version of the Bible.

Excerpts from THE IRRATIONAL SEASON by Madeleine
L'Engle are © 1977 Crosswicks Ltd. Published by Winston-
Seabury Press, Minneapolis, Minnesota. All rights reserved.
Used with permission.

Cover Design: B. J. Osborne
Cover Transparency: Paul Weigle
Book Design: Roy Wallace
First Printing: January, 1986 (5)
Library of Congress Catalog Card Number: 85-52014
ISBN 0-8358-0526-3

Printed in the United States of America

With love and gratitude to the people of the three congregations I have served:

The Otisville-Mt. Hope Presbyterian Church
The First Presbyterian Church of Yorktown
The First Presbyterian Church of Stamford

Because of your warm response to my preaching and my ministry, I am forever in your debt. "I thank my God in all my remembrance of you" (Phil. 1:3).

∽ The ∽ Apostles' Creed

I BELIEVE in God the Father Almighty, maker of heaven and earth;

And in Jesus Christ his only Son our Lord: who was conceived by the Holy Ghost, born of the Virgin Mary, suffered under Pontius Pilate, was crucified, dead, and buried; he descended into hell; the third day he rose again from the dead; he ascended into heaven, and sitteth on the right hand of God the Father Almighty; from thence he shall come to judge the quick and the dead.

I believe in the Holy Ghost, the holy catholic church, the communion of saints, the forgiveness of sins, the resurrection of the body, and the life everlasting. *Amen.*

Contents

Preface

If the reader hears echoes of the pulpit in these chapters on the Apostles' Creed, it is because the pages rise out of parish life, out of the doubts and discoveries of a faith community. This is the original setting. The broad intent is to inform and inspire, to speak to both mind and heart so that the inherent beauty, relevance, and power of Christianity will make its ancient appeal.

More narrowly defined, the intent is to rescue the Creed from being a museum piece, unintelligible religious jargon from the past. To the extent that its language is antique and its theological concepts obscure, it will be more a hindrance than a help to many laypersons. Its use in worship as a faith affirmation will lack force, and its primary importance in Christian history and tradition will go unrecognized by the vast majority of church members. It is my purpose, therefore, to break open the language of the Creed, taking it phrase by phrase, so that the meaning becomes clear. As part of the process, there will be illustration, analogy, comparison, and as careful an explanation of theological terms as I can manage.

The Creed, of course, is more than a piece of abstract theology to be analyzed. It took shape out of faith experience, out of the passionate desire of earlier Christians to live their faith and declare their faith in their own day. It is the crystallization of essential belief and practice. Therefore, as with all the creeds, it has a compelling inner dynamic since it rests on concrete historical experience. The title of the book, *Creed and Christ,* underlines what becomes so apparent in the study of the Apostles' Creed, that it is a creed christo-logical in its center and circumference.

These things being so, some of my intentions come to light:

- To convince the reader of the relevance of the Apostles' Creed.

- To awaken faith in contemporary men and women as they perceive the awakened faith of the church in another day.

- To emphasize the experiential nature of Chris-tianity.

- To make clear that we in the twentieth-century church are linked in an unbroken chain to Christians in the first century, since their con-tagious faith has been passed from generation to generation, making it possible for us today to hear and believe the good news of the gospel.

- To make some small contribution to the vitality of the church today, so that its integrity and inextinguishable joy will lead others to claim our confession as their own, "Jesus Christ is Lord and Savior."

How to Use This Book

Because each chapter is a unit in itself, this book lends itself to group study and discussion. I believe that it will turn loose some lively discussion and do so at depth, if it is given half a chance. Lenten schools of religion, covenant or fellowship groups, Bible studies, adult church school classes, confirmation and church membership classes, men's and women's associations all might find the book useful. Each group participant, or family unit, would have a copy, raise questions, and make observations, marking them in the margins in preparation for the meetings of the group. Questions at the end of each chapter can be used to generate discussion, and they are indicative of the kinds of questions a group might raise. It is a book that will bring people to the exploration of essential questions about faith and about the meaning of Christ for their lives and churches.

A second major use of the book is individual study, reflection, and personal growth. Seasons of the church year, such as Advent, Lent, and Pentecost, would be particularly good times for such reading. Vacation and leisure times and daily times set aside for reading and prayer are further possibilities.

If there is a third major use for the book, it would be as a tool for evangelism. I think that the book readily lends itself to presenting essential Christian truth in a way that will elicit internal dialogue and response.

I hope that those who have responsibility for preaching, teaching, or leading small groups will find some helpful material here.

RON JAMES

1

Introduction

A creed is a belief statement, a confession of faith. That is why the Apostles' Creed begins, "I believe in God," and goes on to list essential elements of belief. It necessarily faces each of us with the question, What do you believe in? Or, to put it another way, What do you affirm as finally significant? By making its own affirmations, the Creed asks, What meaning have you found? What truth do you claim? For what purpose are you living?

Life itself raises these questions. How can anyone help asking what and why when surrounded by an infinite sky? We stand on a minor planet looking out on an ocean of space, expanding, experts tell us, at the speed of light. And we stand here conscious of our own existence. All around is this limitless void, this vast emptiness, and in it we humans, earthlings, islands of consciousness. How in the world did we get here?

Not only are we surrounded by endless space but by endless time, trailing back before our birth in unending duration, aeons, billions of earth years. Out there in front of us, after our death, who knows how many generations are yet to come? Out of the incalculable past we are born on this planet and live out our brief years; then once more infinity closes over us. We are born, we die, and the ages continue to roll.

Do you see what I mean? Life itself raises the questions: Who am I? To what purpose my life? Why this wondrous world, so full of beauty and terror?

Since mystery is so prevalent, meaning becomes precious. When we discover some piece of meaning, some truth about life, it becomes a treasure. We make a symbol so we can remember, mark out a day to celebrate, build an altar to worship, and perhaps write a creed so we can preserve the riches we have found. The Apostles' Creed is such a statement. It is a crisp, crystallized declaration of "things which are most surely believed" (Luke 1:1, KJV). One of my friends calls it "a trellis for faith to climb."

The title, *The Apostles' Creed,* is first found in A.D. 390, in a letter (Epistle 42:5) of Saint Ambrose, one of the notable church leaders. But the roots of the Creed are far earlier. It probably grew out of baptismal questions such as these that date from A.D. 220:

> Do you believe in God the Father Almighty? Do you believe in Jesus Christ, the Son of God, who was born of the Holy Spirit from the virgin Mary and was cru- cified under Pontius Pilate and died and was buried and rose again? . . . Do you believe in the Holy Spirit, the Holy Church, and the resurrection of the dead?[1]

Before A.D. 200, Irenaeus is said to have written: "The church, though dispersed throughout the whole world, has received from the apostles and their disciples this faith. She believes in one God, the Father Almighty, Maker of heaven and earth."

Introduction

This most ancient of the creeds represents the faith of the early church and is drawn from such New Testament passages as Matthew 27:22–33; Matthew 28:19; Acts 8:37; Acts 17:3; First Corinthians 12:3; and First Peter 3:18.

— 2 —

God the Father Almighty, Maker of Heaven and Earth. . .

In the first article of the Creed there are three basic designations for God, placed there in careful order. We will take each in turn.

Father

God is neither male nor female, and all persons, male and female, have an equally important part to play in the church of Jesus Christ. With these important truths in mind, let us examine the biblical use of "Father" as a name for God.

God is referred to as "Father" only fifteen times in the Old Testament—that's a remarkable scarcity! Only once does the literature of the Dead Sea Scrolls call God, "Father." Only four times is God called "Father" in the Apocrypha, those books that fall between the two testaments. Of all the prayers we have from Jewish writers of that day, only two in the first two centuries call God, "Father." He is not addressed as "Father" in Jewish life and worship today.

By contrast, the Gospels record Jesus calling God

"Father" 170 times. "Father" was Jesus' constant form of address when he spoke *to* God or *about* God. "Father" is a wonderful, warming name for God. It is part of the New Testament revelation of who God is.

Perhaps we can draw a conclusion: This Creed, at its heart, at its core, in its nature, is christological. Jesus is its center and circumference. When it begins by calling God "Father," we see the person of Christ, for "Father" is Jesus' basic name for God.

Having seen this, we need to ask in what sense is God the Father? Let's go back to 1545 for an answer, to John Calvin's Catechism of the Church of Geneva. Among other things, this catechism talks about the Apostles' Creed. After quoting the first article, "I believe in God the Father Almighty," the catechism asks, "Why do you call him Father?" And answers, "Primarily with regard to Christ, who is his eternal wisdom, begotten of him before all time, and who, being sent into the world, was declared his Son."[1] It is true, therefore, as Karl Barth observes, that "the whole Creed refers to our knowledge of God in Jesus Christ. Jesus Christ does not appear in the second act only. He is unceasingly present, unceasingly active."[2]

When the Apostles' Creed calls God "Father," the primary meaning is the Father of our Lord Jesus Christ. The letters to the Romans, Corinthians, and Colossians, all include the phrase "the God and Father of our Lord Jesus Christ."

Let's take it a step further. If we affirm that God, indeed, is the Father of our Lord Jesus Christ, then what? What follows? What conclusion do we reach? Simply, truly, and wonderfully that God is our Father, too.

Hear the Heidelberg Catechism: "What believest thou when thou sayest, 'I believe in God the Father

Almighty, Maker of heaven and earth'?" And the answer: "That the eternal Father of our Lord Jesus Christ, who . . . made heaven and earth . . . is, for the sake of Christ His Son, my God and my Father."[3] Do you believe this? Do you believe that at the heart of this cold universe there is a loving Father who "treasures up his bright designs and works his sovereign will"?[4] Do you believe that behind the mysteries inhabiting infinity, giving birth to human life, is a loving Father? That this is his world? That you are his child? You declare it every time you repeat in the Apostles' Creed, "I believe in God the Father Almighty."

The Creed is more than an intellectual formulation; it is a witness to experience. It does not propose ideas for our minds to master but sets forth a truth that can transform and master us, as it did the first Christians. When it says that God is our Father, it points us toward an experience of this love, points us toward relationship with this loving God. Here is One who broods over our lives, One to whom we are accountable, yet One who forgives every failure. Here is One who sends us into the world to make our own way, yet One who walks every step with us. Here is One who claims our unswerving loyalty and who is unwaveringly loyal and loving to us. God tenderly cares for us, waits patiently for us to return when we wander, holds open the door of home. No wonder Jesus called God by the intimate name, *Abba,* which means "Dear Father of mine."

Almighty

This is the Creed's second designation for God, the Father who is almighty. What goes through your mind when I say that? What image do you see? What picture do you paint of God the Almighty? Maybe you remember words from the hymn, "He plants his footsteps in the sea, and rides upon the storm."[5] Maybe you see a towering vision of God who is a thousand stories high, leaning forward on the great white throne, with blinding rays of energy emanating from face and form like lightning, penetrating every corner of the universe, controlling all creation.

One could spin out many fancies. One could wade into the deep waters of philosophical theology or engage in endless speculation about how God is almighty. But this is not what the Bible does nor what the Creed does. The biblical view is that God is almighty in the way the divine self is revealed to us and the divine will is accomplished through us. I said before that the three designations for God in this first article of the Creed are in careful order. By the order of the Creed, *we are to understand how God is almighty only as we understand how God is the Father.* The Creed does not say, "Almighty God the Father" but rather "God the Father Almighty." God's omnipotence is to be seen from the perspective of fatherly love.

Take Jacob as an example of this truth. Notice the sequence of revelation in Genesis 35:9–15. First, God appears to Jacob at a place called Paddan-aram and blesses him. The meeting and the blessing effect a change in Jacob, and he is given a new name as a sign of the change. He is no longer Jacob; he is Israel, a name that means "God rules." Then and only then, on the basis of that encounter, that meeting, and that change of heart and life, does God say, "I am God Almighty." This becomes the basis for the command to obedience and task, "Be fruitful and multiply; a nation and a company of nations shall come from you" (v. 11).

We experience something similar in our luminous moments, our moments of spiritual experience with God, when it is revealed to us that God is almighty.

Almighty in what sense? God is the Lord, we are in God's hand, life finds meaning in him, and death brings us to him. Ultimately God is all that matters and all we have. Revelation records the unforgettable statement: " 'I am the Alpha and the Omega,' says the Lord God, who is and who was and who is to come, the Almighty" (1:8). More directly yet—and this is what the Creed means—God is almighty in that God is given to us in Jesus Christ. Karl Barth has said:

> In Jesus Christ, God, out of the mercifulness of his heart, comes down from eternity. . . . He bears all sins, all miseries and even death. He wills to suffer in his Son, and bearing in him all our sins, he wills to glorify himself. Victorious through the Cross, that is his almightiness.[6]

God is the Father and is almighty.

Maker of Heaven and Earth

In the third designation of this first article of the Creed we see that God is maker of heaven and earth. That God is the Creator is the Creed's primary example of God's almightiness. God is the source of all that spreads out before the human eye in such grandeur. "Heaven and earth," says the Creed, meaning the totality of things—sky, stars, earth, water, growing things, living things. Nothing is beyond the reach of God's creative power. All things find their origin in God.

These days much is being written about the web of the universe, the interrelatedness of this far-flung cosmos. Fritjof Capra writes:

> The universe is no longer seen as a machine, made up of a multitude of objects, but has to be pictured as one

indivisible, dynamic whole whose parts are essentially interrelated and can be understood only as patterns of a cosmic process.[7]

Studies in the new physics, in psychology, in medicine, indicate the profound unity of the world and of the human mind and body. As early as 1930, James Jeans, British physicist, wrote:

> Today there is a wide measure of agreement . . . that the stream of knowledge is heading towards a non-mechanical reality; the universe begins to look more like a great thought than a great machine.[8]

Fascinating as this line of reasoning may be, one must readily admit that the world by no means perfectly reflects God. It is at best a broken mirror, full of light and darkness, joy and pain, promise and frustration, life and death. It is impossible to reason from the world itself to a loving, almighty Father. One can only move in the opposite direction, as does the Creed, from a Father who chooses to be revealed to us to the world as the work of the Father's hands. Hebrews puts it clearly, "By faith we understand that the world was created by the word of God" (11:3).

It is the biblical view that God created the world to be separate from its Creator, that though the whole created order is subject to God's word and will, God stands apart from it. It is the biblical view as well that it is a fallen creation, full of brokenness and pain, in rebellion from the loving purposes of its Maker. From Genesis to Revelation, from the tree of the knowledge of good and evil to the tree of life whose leaves are for the healing of the nations, the Bible tells of God's grand design for the restoration of the whole creation. To this end God calls a people, Israel, to bear his name and sends the Christ to redeem a fallen humanity. All who hear and respond to this call are to be agents of the restoration.

Once more, as before, the truth is personal. God is not merely the Creator in abstraction, in theory, or as a postulate. God is *my* Creator, who has placed me here for a reason—to be open to God's will, to place myself and all my powers at God's disposal, to join in the redemptive purpose for all creation. This Creator is the God I confess in the Creed when I say, "I believe in God the Father Almighty, maker of heaven and earth."

Questions for Reflection

1. How does belief centered in the mind relate to belief centered in the heart? How does faith progress from the theoretical to the personal?

2. How do you feel about God being called "Father"?

3. In what sense is God "almighty" for you?

4. In the light of this opening statement from the Creed, what would you teach your children or grandchildren about God?

5. In what specific ways are your commitments and actions affected by your belief in "God the Father Almighty"?

3

Jesus Christ His Only Son Our Lord . . .

Let me say it again, a creed is a belief statement. In any given generation the church may choose to write a creed. It studies scripture and seeks to grasp the meaning and mood of its culture. Then it speaks to the intersection of its culture and its scripture by writing a creed. It says to its own members and to the secular world, "This we believe!"

There is power in belief statements. When a well-known author, scientist, or musician writes an article, "This I Believe," in a magazine, a lot of people read it. They want to know what that person considers to be finally significant in life.

However, we hear so many softminded, puny belief statements that we become jaded. You know the kind I mean. "A movie star extols the virtues of a product and states the deficiencies of its competitor. Radio, television, and magazine ads assault us with a barrage of these "I believe my product is superior" statements. Advertising agencies have tried to cash in on the power of belief statements.

Some popular music contains absolute gems of softmindedness. Think about the words to the song "I Believe." Sentimental? Yes! Substantial? Hardly. If you want a substantial statement in music, listen for the theme and variations in Beethoven's *Ninth Symphony,* in Tchaikovsky's *1812 Overture,* or in Brahms's *Violin Concerto in D Major.*

One more observation about creeds: They are not just religious talk. They are built on and arise from the basic conviction of the church in the generation in which they are written. They are not made of wood, hay, and stubble but are forged in steel and carved from rock. Often they have been paid for in blood. Lines from Albert Camus make my point, lines rising from his participation in the French Resistance Movement during World War II: "One really possesses only what one has paid for. We have paid dearly, and we have not finished paying. But we have our certainties."[1]

Now on to the second article of the Creed, "I believe . . . in Jesus Christ his only Son our Lord." As signposts through the exploration of this theme, I choose four ideas: The church believes in Jesus because he *rescues, reveals, reflects,* and *rules.*

Rescues

In the small Italian port city of Portofino, fishermen have placed a large statue of Jesus underwater at the harbor entrance. There he stands, this Christ of the depths, arms upraised in blessing upon every boat passing overhead. But there is a problem. Seaweed, algae, and crustaceans cling to the statue, obscuring the face and form of Christ. So once each year divers go down with wire brushes to scrub the lines clear once more.

The application is obvious: In the ebb and flow of life, the clear biblical portrait of Christ can become blurred and indistinct. We no longer see his face. Then we need to seek him at the source once more, in the sometimes disturbing clarity of the New Testament. For example, when Jesus asks, "Who do you say that I am?" (Matt. 16:15), Peter's magnificent response is to be the church's in every generation, "You are the Christ, the Son of the living God" (v. 16).

This second article of the Creed can remove the accumulated layers of neglect, doubt, and misunderstanding that obscure the face of Christ for us all. Look at the name "Jesus." It is the Greek form of the Hebrew *Joshua* ("God saves"). It is the name God's messenger revealed to Joseph, the husband of Mary: "You shall call his name Jesus, for he will save his people from their sins" (Matt. 1:21). In his life Jesus fulfilled the meaning of his name. In him God rescues people.

In one very real sense this rescue is *from* something. The traditional and biblical answer is "saved from our sins." Yes, that's right! Rescued from guilt, from the torment of a restless conscience, from the chains with which our past life can bind us and crush our joy. To be saved is to be rescued by God from the confining bondage of meaninglessness and from the depressing futility of our swiftly passing years. It is to be rescued from our fear of death and the dark unknown. Jesus is the Savior, and in him we know ourselves to be sought after, found, and forgiven by God. "What man of you," asks Jesus, "having a hundred sheep, if he has lost one of them, does not leave the ninety-nine in the wilderness, and go after the one which is lost, until he finds it? And when he has found it, he lays it on his shoulders, rejoicing" (Luke 15:4–5).

But it is not just rescue *from,* it is rescue *for.*

Christianity is not a safe harbor religion, so that we can furl our sails, duck out of all the storms, and lie quietly at anchor. It is a ship built for the high seas, for adventure, for full sail, for new horizons. The imposing, and often forbidding, word *salvation* means "wholeness, health, fulfillment, and completion." We are saved so we can organize the scattered forces of our personalities around the glowing center of Christ and allow God, through him, to begin within us the process of transformation. In that process we are called to serve the Lord of the kingdom, to love, to help, to give, to introduce others to the Savior, to keep alive the rumor that God is in our land.

I believe in Jesus the Savior. He rescues.

Reveals

This second article of the Creed puts the two names together, Jesus Christ. If we were to state it more clearly, we would say, "I believe . . . in Jesus the Christ." Christ is not really a name but a title, a designation, a claim about the nature of the man Jesus. The carpenter's son, Mary's son, Jesus of Nazareth is the man. Christ is the Messiah, the Son of God.

A little background may be helpful here. *Christ* is a Greek word that literally means, "the anointed one." Its roots are deeply embedded in Old Testament soil, where the king of Israel was called "God's anointed." He was anointed with oil by a priest or prophet to show that he had been chosen by God to bear the office. It was a sign that the presence and power of God were with him. Then, as the major prophets—Isaiah, Jeremiah, Ezekiel—begin to write, they tell of the coming of a great King, One who becomes the central figure in the unfolding biblical drama. He will come in the last days, he will reveal God's glory, and he will establish God's everlasting kingdom. All these things have been hidden, but in the Christ, the anointed one, they will be revealed. To put it another way, Christ is God's declared intention to make himself known to the world.

This is right at the center of what Christians believe. Allow me to spend a little time, therefore, in honing it to a finer edge. Christianity does not begin with an idea, no matter how lofty. Christianity does not begin with a theory, no matter how finely spun. Christianity does not begin with an abstraction, no matter how poetic. Christianity begins with a person, an actual, factual, historical, tangible, human, believable person, Jesus of Nazareth, whom we confess to be the Christ. He is, in T. S. Eliot's words, "still point of the turning world." For Christians, he is hub, center, focus, window on the face of God.

All well and good, this abstract God, not much discomfort in that. Star Maker, Cosmic Architect, First Cause, we can argue this over coffee or in study sessions. But a human Jesus, carpenter of Nazareth, who wandered the length and breadth of Israel teaching and healing, that's another matter. Two thousand years ago, sure, but still a little close for comfort. Here is One who does not pose theoretical questions about a distant or impersonal God but calls us to accountability before One whose inescapable presence is the very ground of our existence. God is there "if I make my bed in Sheol" or "if I take the wings of the morning and dwell in the uttermost parts of the sea" (Psalm 139:8–9). I am faced with inevitable questions: Who am I in relation to this God? What do I believe about this eternal Spirit who stands at every crossroad of my life?

According to C. S. Lewis:

An impersonal God—well and good. A subjective God of beauty, truth and goodness, inside our own heads—better still. A formless life-force surging through us, a vast power which we can tap—best of all. But God Himself, alive, pulling at the other end of the cord, perhaps approaching at an infinite speed, the hunter, king, husband—that is quite another matter. . . . There comes a moment when people who have been dabbling in religion . . . suddenly draw back. Supposing we really found Him? [Did we bargain for that when we joined the church?] . . . Worse still, supposing He had found us?[2]

Reflects

This brings us to the idea that Jesus reflects the very nature of God. That is what the Creed means when it calls Jesus "his only Son." What do we mean when we make this confession? For one thing, we hear and repeat Peter's confession, "You are the Christ, the Son of the living God" (Matt. 16:16). The disciples, who knew him most intimately, stood most in awe of him and, with mingled love and adoration, acknowledged in him a divine authority. In him they felt the very presence of their God and gave him the supreme name "Messiah."[3] The apostle John wrote that he was "full of grace and truth; we have beheld his glory, glory as of the only Son from the Father" (John 1:14). Peter said, "We were eyewitnesses of his majesty," (2 Pet. 1:16).

Jesus is the only Son of God; he reflects God as truly as a mirror reflects someone's image. In a human parallel, think of a woman looking in a mirror. It is not the person herself, this image in the mirror, yet it *is* the person herself. It is so truly that person that we can say, "Yes, there is Martha in the glass. She looks like Martha, acts like Martha, speaks like Martha, and is, in fact, Martha herself—but in reflection. It is Martha, yet is reflects truly the real Martha." Just so, Jesus is the reflection of God. He is the only Son of God.

The Creed tells us this: In Jesus the one true God is present, not a second God, not a demigod, not a godly man, but God. As Hans Küng says, "Our whole redemption depends on the fact that in Jesus we are concerned with the God who is really God."[4] To put it in the image of Karl Barth, "Jesus Christ is not only God's interpreter, he is the very text to be interpreted."[5] In a sermon Ernest Campbell said, "I find in Jesus all I could ever, should ever, need ever mean by God."[6] And Tom Driver wrote, "[The disciples] did not declare that this Gallilean had *spoken* the Word of God. They said plainly that the divine *logos* is what he *was*."[7]

What does this mean for us, that Jesus is God's only Son? It means that our decision for faith in God inevitably moves through the person of Jesus. He is the way. The way we understand him, experience him, come to terms with him, is the way we come to terms with God. He is *El Camino Real,* the royal road. He makes God tangible, puts us in touch, opens for us, as the New Testament says, "the new and living way" (Heb. 10:20). Whatever of the face of God we will be permitted to see in the world to come, will be because Jesus is the human face of God, and on his face, his beautiful, majestic, loving face, we see reflected the glory and love of God.

Rules

So Jesus rescues, he reveals, and he reflects God. He also rules. "I believe . . . in Jesus Christ his only Son our Lord." This title, "Lord," is a weighty one. There are so many pieces of shining truth here that it is hard to know where to begin. Jesus is Lord. What does that mean? John Calvin answers, "In that he was appointed by the Father to have us under his power."[8]

The Heidelberg Catechism asks, "Wherefore callest thou Him our Lord?" And answers,

> Because He hath redeemed us, both soul and body, from all our sins, not with gold and silver, but with His precious blood, and hath delivered us from all the power of the devil; and thus hath made us His own property.[9]

Obviously, then, Jesus is our Lord in that he has paid the price for our salvation; therefore, he becomes our ultimate authority to whom we owe both love and loyalty unto death. He is, as the disciples called him, "Master," although not in the sense of keeping us in bondage. Only in the glorious liberty of the gospel, with a joyful, liberating obedience, do we call him "Lord." In him rests our destiny and hope of eternal life.

This title, this ascription, "Lord," does not simply mean "Sir." Nor is it merely a title of nobility, as in British use, Lord William Hilary Higgenbotham. It is far more. When the Old Testament was translated into Greek about 250 B.C., the Hebrew letters for Yahweh were translated by the Greek word *kurios,* which is the word we translate as "Lord." To speak of the lordship of Jesus Christ is to speak of his divinity. That's why the Creed says, "his [God's] only son our Lord." And that's why the Nicene Creed states that Jesus is "of one substance with the Father," who is "God of God, Light of Light, very God of very God."

Nowhere does the New Testament deal more powerfully with the word *Lord,* than in Philippians 2:9–11:

Therefore God has highly exalted him and bestowed on
him the name which is above every name, that at the
name of Jesus every knee should bow . . . and every
tongue confess that Jesus Christ is Lord, to the glory of
God the Father.

"Jesus Christ is Lord" was the earliest Christian
confession. In these words are the sum and substance of
our Christian faith. In a day when all citizens were
forced to bend the knee and confess, "Caesar is Lord,"
Christians refused, and their courage, their conviction,
their boundless joy and love, the contagion of their faith
in this Jesus, were a fresh wind of the Spirit of God
blowing across that decaying empire.

Shall not we Christians, in our own day, a day of the
fear of a nuclear holocaust, a day of devotion to false
idols—Mars the god of war, Narcissus the image of
vanity, Midas the man of wealth, Dionysus the god of
wine—shall not we confess in our world that "Jesus
Christ is Lord"?

He rescues, he reveals, he reflects, he rules.[10] How
much is in this compact sentence, "I believe . . . in Jesus
Christ his only Son our Lord."

Questions for Reflection

1. Is it true in your own expression of Christian faith, or that of your church, that it is easier to talk about God than about Jesus? Why?

2. Ask yourself, "If I were to begin each day with the affirmation, 'Jesus Christ is Lord,' in what specific ways could that change my day?"

3. How does your relationship with Jesus Christ affect your relationship with family, friends, strangers?

4. How could your church help people to know and experience the truth in this "article of belief"?

4

Conceived by the Holy Ghost, Born of the Virgin Mary . . .

This chapter could well bear the title, "The Birth of Jesus," since it rises from the creedal statement, "conceived by the Holy Ghost, born of the Virgin Mary." Why is this affirmation about Jesus' birth placed at this particular point in the Creed, following the statement, "Jesus Christ his only Son our Lord"? It is here in answer to two questions. First, in what sense is Jesus Christ the only Son of God? The answer is that he is God's Son because God was present in the man Jesus of Nazareth to such a degree that he was God's self-expression, God's very self in human flesh and blood. Second, how is he our Lord? The answer is that he is our Lord because he took upon himself our human nature and was born among us from a human mother, so that he is fully human, truly man.

Have you ever tried to think through what this means? At its heart, Christianity is not an intellectual formulation. It is not theory, philosophy, metaphysics, or ethics. *It is an event!* Matthew's words are familiar to us all: "Jesus was born in Bethlehem of Judea in the days of Herod the king" (2:1). Long ago and far away, yes; in another land, yes; but in our world, this world where we live out our days and years, on our own turf, we might say. Hear the wonder of the early church: "In many and various ways God spoke of old to our fathers by the prophets; but in these last days he has spoken to us by a Son" (Heb. 1:1–2).

Now let's examine these two phrases from the Creed.

Conceived by the Holy Ghost

In the phrase "conceived by the Holy Ghost," *ghost* is simply another word for *spirit* and comes from linguistic backgrounds that have to do with breath, wind, life-force, enlivening principle. Thus, Holy Ghost means Holy Spirit.

Let me quote Karl Barth again, for I am indebted to his book, *The Faith of the Church:*

> "Conceived by the Holy Ghost," means that Jesus, in the sense of the Creed and the early Church alike, was God, with no reservation and no ambiguity. In Christ it is God himself who became man, and not a half-god, not an appearance of God. The existence of Jesus is the manifestation of God's existence.[1]

That's a pretty big bite of theology, so let's look at it more carefully. Jesus was conceived by the Holy Ghost. What does the Creed, and behind it the New Testament, intend this to mean? That God's own nature, God's own person and power, God's very self, are so woven into Jesus' soul and psyche that he is inseparable from God and is God's Son. "I and the Father are one" is the way John's Gospel (10:30) put it. In trying to state how Jesus is "only Son of God," John said, "And the Word became flesh and dwelt among us" (1:14). Jesus is the Word of God in living form, that is, he is God's self-expression.

He is God saying, being, doing what God wishes to say to us, be for us, and accomplish through us.

E. Stanley Jones wrote a book of daily devotional readings, *The Word Became Flesh*. The entire opening page is a picture of Jesus, arms outstretched, saying, "Come unto me, all ye that labour and are heavy laden, and I will give you rest." When you look very, very closely, you see that the picture is made entirely of words. A Korean artist has written the whole New Testament on a six foot by four foot piece of canvas— 185,000 words. The figure of Jesus is not imposed on the words but rises out of the words, which are inked light and dark to reveal the picture.

So, out of the words of the New Testament rises the living Word, God's self-expression in human form. The words themselves make visible this living Word, Jesus, the Word become flesh. No wonder William Barclay wrote, "It might well be held that this is the greatest single verse in the whole New Testament."[2] E. Stanley Jones remarked that this is the great divide between Christianity and the world religions. Not that they do not have truth, not that they lack noble sentiments, gracious teaching, or gifted leaders. But in them, said Jones, it is a Word become word—a system, a moralism, a religious framework.[3] For Christianity alone, the Word became flesh; in a way that we can never capture in human words, God came among us in Jesus, opened his heart to us in Jesus, gave his life for us in Jesus, overcame death for us in Jesus, unlocking the gates of the eternal kingdom.

Whenever churches do not know this, feel this, live this, proclaim and teach this, they miss the way. By their divorce from the New Testament's engagement with the living Word, they fail to be what the church must be in every generation, the community of Jesus.

Born of the Virgin Mary

Here is the pattern of these two phrases in the Apostles' Creed. "Conceived by the Holy Ghost" means Jesus is God. "Born of the Virgin Mary" means Jesus is human. These are the two natures of Jesus in one person that the church can never fully explain but must always maintain. We can talk around it, we can draw analogies, but we can never really capture it in a creed, for in the final analysis it is an irreducible mystery. "Conceived by the Holy Ghost" is the mystery of the incarnation. "Born of the Virgin Mary" is the sign of the mystery.

I don't see how I can write about this theme without observing that a great many people are unable to take the virgin birth stories in Matthew and Luke literally. Among such people are a great many of the laity and the clergy in both the Roman Catholic and Protestant traditions. For all those who have this struggle, let me point out some things. First, this is not a critically important teaching. It is mentioned only in Matthew and Luke in the New Testament. Mark, John, Paul, and Peter do not speak of it. If it were critically important, as is the death of Christ, his resurrection, his teaching about the kingdom of God, then it would not have gone unmentioned in the rest of the New Testament.

Second, Jesus' being the Son of God does not depend on the virgin birth the way a building depends on its cornerstone or the way the whole Christian gospel depends on the resurrection. If you want authentication of his being the Son of God, then look to his preaching and teaching, the perfection of his life, his own claims about his relationship to God, the sign of his power over the realms of darkness as evidenced by the events of Good Friday and Easter.

Third, our standing before God, our salvation, certainly does not depend on whether or not we accept this teaching literally. There is room for difference here within the Christian family, and God, in loving mercy toward and boundless knowledge of human creatures, will rule no one in or out of the kingdom on the basis of this teaching alone. I have an idea that the critical questions will be more along these lines: Do you know God's love in Jesus? Did you seek to make him known?

After all, what is important in the final analysis is our common Christian confession, "Jesus Christ is Lord and Savior." Anyone who can make that confession, and be bound to Christ in that allegiance, is my sister or brother in faith.

I want to look more closely at this person we name Virgin Mary. As a Protestant, I had never thought much about her. Roman Catholics, it seemed to me, had venerated her right out of her humanness and spun such a web of theology around her that I found her inaccessible. Queen of Heaven, Co-Redemptrix of the human race, Mother of God—these titles were simply too big. And the late dogmas—that she was conceived without sin (1854), that she was taken up bodily into heaven without dying (1950)—these declarations, without biblical weight—were simply puzzling. Nor could I, nor can I, see any reason for praying to Mary. She is not divine, nor semidivine, like some fourth member of the Godhead. She is a beautiful, devoted daughter of Israel, a tenderhearted, spiritually centered peasant girl of Galilee, whom God chose above all others of her day to bear Jesus, the Christ. What an honor! She is, then, a model of motherhood and of receptivity to the word and will of God.

Yet if Catholics have venerated Mary to the skies, Protestants have gone to the opposite extreme of prejudice and neglect. Stay with me for a minute, and let me say something about the Protestant ethos, its mood and character. Historians speculate that the Industrial Revolution would have been later, or different, were it not for the Protestant Reformation. That reformation and that revolution go together and have fostered what we might call the values of the Western world. See if you don't think the following characterize our way of life: science, rational proof, technology, aggressiveness, laissez-faire, rugged individualism. I'm not saying that these are necessarily bad. In fact, they have given us incalculable benefits in wealth and creature comfort. But they are, in some ways, a triumph of the head over the heart. They have made reason king, neglecting emotion and the inner life. By their nature, they are competitive values and emphases, active, forward moving. They seek to make a conquest of nature and to overcome obstacles. They are, therefore, the triumph of the masculine over the feminine. Protestantism, it seems to me, has strong masculine overtones. Of course, many of these things are good, but perhaps we need to consider the other side.

Why has the cult of Mary endured the centuries? Why has human devotion to her been so wholehearted? What need does she fill? What neglected side of the nature of God does she represent? Does she not, in fact, represent the feminine side of the nature of God, a God who is neither masculine nor feminine? Mary becomes an archetypal symbol of the feminine. What does that mean? She represents receptivity, that which is open, centered, and at rest. She represents the need within us all to receive, to be fruitful vessels of God, to be filled with the presence of God so that the Christ is born within us. It is the yieldedness of Mary, her receptivity to the word and will of God, that has caused the church to love her throughout the centuries. There will be a great cost, but she makes the commitment. She does not understand what it will mean, but she hears and obeys the message of God. Her reason holds her back, but her heart draws her forward so that she speaks her unforgettable "Yes!" to God: "Let it be to me according to your word" (Luke 1:38). Madeleine L'Engle writes:

> This is the irrational season
> When love blooms bright and wild.
> Had Mary been filled with reason
> There'd have been no room for the child.[4]

Let me be quick to add that to be receptive is not merely to be passive, nor to surrender your own power, and so become weak. To be receptive does not demand self-abnegation. On the contrary, Mary's receptivity is an offering, a gift, requiring strength and self-possession. Nor is receptivity simply a feminine trait. Each person must cultivate receptivity as part of the journey toward wholeness—openness to God and others, the receiving into oneself of God and others.

On the other side, all of us, men and women alike, need to move outward from our center—to touch others, to exercise our gifts, to be active, to make our impression on the world for Jesus' sake, to live fully and unafraid. Are these not two halves of a whole, receptivity and activity? Are not both simply human traits to be experienced and owned by both men and women?

Because of her willingness to receive the presence of God, Mary became the mother of Jesus, who is the Christ. Because of what God did though Mary, in Jesus, we know we are not forever doomed to strain our eyes upward for some glimpse of God. We are nourished and filled with hope by words spoken with lips like our own. Here is One who is "flesh of our flesh and bone of our bone," One "born of the Virgin Mary."

I conclude with these words of Madeline L'Engle:

> One evening Tallis and I were talking, after teaching a class together. One of the students had been defining God, and everybody agreed that this is impossible. But I said afterwards to Tallis, "*We* can't define God, but didn't God define himself for us, in Jesus Christ?"[5]

In Jesus Christ, God came among us, truly God and truly human, "conceived by the Holy Ghost, born of the Virgin Mary."

Questions for Reflection

1. In what sense is Jesus born in the human heart?

2. Discuss Mary's struggle in being receptive to God's word. Then discuss your own struggle.

3. Try to describe one instance in which, like Mary, your faith was demonstrated in openness and receptivity.

4. In your experience, is the church an open and receptive community?

5

Suffered under Pontius Pilate, Was Crucified, Dead, and Buried; He Descended into Hell . . .

A good approach to the Apostles' Creed requires more than the assent of the mind and the experience of the heart. There must be an act of the will too. One decides to become a Christian, to be and remain a Christian. Let me quote some words from Sheldon Vanauken that illustrate my point:

> One can only choose a side . . . I now choose my side . . . I confess my doubts and ask my Lord Christ to enter my life. I do not *know* God is, I do but say: Be it unto me according to Thy will. I do not affirm that I am without doubt, I do but ask for help, having chosen to overcome it. I do but say: Lord I believe—help Thou mine unbelief.[1]

One does not become a Christian, after all, because the whole creed can be repeated without a shadow of doubt. One becomes and remains a Christian by a choice to do so. Nor is it purely an intellectual choice. Not at all! It is a choice that touches the whole range of human experience—love, loneliness, need, fear, sickness and mortality, meaning and purpose, the spiritual hunger and thirst within—all these things are involved. Somehow, somewhere, someday each of us is faced with the inevitable question, and the inevitable choice, Who and what is God in my life? Where are you? Begin with the things you can affirm, "Lord, I believe . . . ," and go on from there, "Help my unbelief." Are you willing to take the risk?

This chapter brings us to a belief statement about the suffering and death of Christ. Listen to the Creed, "conceived by the Holy Ghost, born of the Virgin Mary, suffered under Pontius Pilate." It's so familiar that we don't hear the contrast. "Born of the Virgin Mary, suffered under Pontius Pilate." What? Nothing between those two phrases? Do we move so quickly from the birth to the death? What about the intervening years? Thirty-three of them, weren't there? Do they deserve no mention at all? How immediate and direct the contrast, how abrupt, even abrasive. Obviously, moving so quickly toward it, the Creed is intensely concerned with the death of Jesus.

Suffered

In his passion, that is, in his trial and death, Jesus suffered. We all know the story of the whip, the crown of thorns, the ridicule, the hammer and nails, the searing sun, the thirst, the spear thrust. But the suffering is broader than that. From the beginning, the very beginning, he suffers. He has a stable for a birthing room. Herod hears of the birth of a new king and sends soldiers to seek and slay the son of Mary.

At the beginning of his ministry, the Gospels show the rising opposition of the religious leaders. After Jesus heals a paralytic in the synagogue at Capernaum on the

Sabbath, "The Pharisees went out, and immediately held counsel with the Herodians against him, how to destroy him" (Mark 3:6). He is a puzzle to his mother and an offense to his brothers and sisters. They simply do not understand what he is doing, and they fear for his life. He himself says, "The Son of man must suffer many things, and be rejected . . . and be killed" (Mark 8:31). In many ways he is a stranger among his own people—politically, socially, religiously—he does not seem to fit in. The crowds who follow him at the beginning forsake him at the end. The Palm Sunday multitudes who hail him with their "Hallelujahs" condemn him a few days later with their cries for crucifixion. One of his own disciples, Judas, betrays him. Another, Peter, denies him three times. The rest run away. He is arrested by the leaders of his own nation, who manage to enlist their conquerors, the Romans, to put him on trial, and through a series of nimble political maneuvers, they bring about his crucifixion.

What is going on here? How can these things be? Why is there such a tide of rejection moving against Jesus? It is in the very nature of the world to make Jesus suffer, a world with a different set of values, a world on a different course of action, a world tuned to different realities. What kind of world? A world inescapably entangled in violence, where might makes right; a world inextricably mired in self-concern, where self-advantage takes precedence over all. A man *against* violence, a man *for* others, is going to suffer in such a world.

How does Jesus make his point? How does he tell his story? By suffering. He does not make his point, as some wished he would, by calling down fire from heaven to annihilate his enemies. He chooses another way, which turns out to be the way of the cross. Jesus, like the rabbis of his day, chooses to model his teaching. He chooses a seldom-used theme of the Old Testament and makes that central. It is the theme of the Suffering Servant, through whom Israel is redeemed. In a book called *Night,* Elic Wiesel writes:

> The SS hanged two Jewish man and a youth in front of the whole camp. The men died quickly, but the death throes of the youth lasted for half an hour. "Where is God? Where is he?" someone asked behind me. As the youth still hung in torment in the noose after a long time, I heard the man call again, "Where is God now?" And I heard a voice in myself answer: "Where is he? He is here. He is hanging there on the gallows."[2]

For Christians this is the figure of Isaiah 53, "despised and rejected," the one who is "oppressed" and "afflicted" and, in the sacrifice of his life, "makes himself an offering for sin." He is brought to shame and death, "although he had done no violence, and there was no deceit in his mouth." In dying he accomplishes deliverance for those who are held in bondage to violence, selfishness, and death. Through him, God's kingdom will come.

He "suffered under Pontius Pilate." What power there is in his suffering! Gandhi illustrated this force in India, as did Martin Luther King, Jr., in the United States. Those who are willing to suffer, taking their stand with Christ, can bring about deliverance for others.

What does it mean, for each of us, that Christ suffered? It means that he hears not only your praise but also your pain. When life goes into a tailspin, when you fail and weep out your agony into your pillow, when you feel utterly alone, when you curse life, yourself, and those around you and feel God has forsaken you, Jesus knows. He will stand with you until the pain has been softened and transformed into beauty of soul.

Why is Pontius Pilate mentioned in the Creed? To anchor it to history. A few years ago a group of us were in Israel, and we visited the ancient seaport city of Caesarea. There, standing right out in the open along one of the walkways, is a stone unearthed by archaeologists that bears the inscription, "Pontius Pilate, Prefect of Judea." Jesus suffered under Pontius Pilate.

Crucified

The writers of the New Testament, and with them Christians over the centuries, have never escaped the shock of the statement, "He was crucified!" On a Roman cross, an instrument of execution reserved for murderers and traitors, Jesus Christ, God's only Son our Lord, was put to death brutally, ignominiously, thorns jammed down on his head, hands and feet nailed to the wood, hanging there suspended between heaven and earth. No wonder Negro slaves sang:

> O my Lord, don't you
> hear that hammer ringin',
> Surely he died on Calvary!

Crucifixion was not a pleasant way to die. Victims would often linger for three days or more, experiencing thirst, exhaustion, and searing pain, seeing the crowds who came to jeer, mock, or merely stare. Cicero called crucifixion "that most cruel and terrifying punishment." No citizen could be crucified, but Rome employed this terrible death as a common form of execution for enemies of the empire. The Roman general, Varus, for instance, crucified two thousand insurgents along the Appian Way.

Hear the astonishment and wonder of these words:

> Christ Jesus, who, though he was in the form of God,
> did not count equality with God a thing to be grasped,
> but emptied himself, taking the form of a servant,
> being born in [human] likeness. . . . He humbled him-
> self and became obedient unto death, even death on a
> cross.
>
> —Philippians 2:5–8.

Think of it! Nineteen-and-a-half centuries later, people in a land halfway around the world, in an age of nuclear power, place that same sign at the center of their worship space. What a mark it has left on our world! What a place it holds in Christian consciouness! We may forget everything else about Christianity, but we remember that Jesus Christ was crucified. He was condemned, scourged, battered, beaten, bruised, burdened with his own cross, and crucified on a barren little hill in Jerusalem called "the place of a skull."

We would have long since forgotten, the sands of time would long since have erased the memory, were it not for a cross and a prayer, the Lord's Prayer. The cross means this: *He died for us.* Wait! Narrow it down. *He died for me.* Peter put it plainly, "He himself bore our sins in his body on the tree" (1 Pet. 2:24). The New Testament says it over and over again—crucified *for us,* in our stead, on our behalf. For what reason? For our awakening to God's love, for our forgiveness and eternal life, for our service for Jesus' sake.

Whatever else Christian faith means, however else we talk about God, whatever else the Bible says or church history reveals, it remains true that the cross alone is our theology. All rises from this center. It is not true that might makes right, that power over others is the last word, or that self-advantage is the bottom line. The bottom line is this, that "God so loved the world that he gave his only Son, that whoever believes in him should not perish but have eternal life" (John 3:16).

The church cannot be the church until it is grasped by the word of the cross, which is the word of sacrificial love. Nor can it be the church until it reflects the nature of the man on the cross, Jesus, God's suffering servant. When all is said and done, the church is the community that speaks out and acts out the compassionate love of its Lord, taking its place with all "who labor and are heavy laden" (Matt. 11:28).

Dead and Buried

What finality! No symbolic death, this. No make-believe death, this. He died, no mistake about it, no shadow of doubt. He died a human death, felt the dark close over him, knew in his bones the universal "No" that death speaks to every daughter and son of Adam. An unknown writer said it well:

> He died!
> And with Him perished all that [we] hold dear;
> Hope lay beside Him in the sepulchre,
> Love grew corse cold, and all things beautiful beside,
>   Died, when He died!

Consider the word *buried*. Somebody may say, "Hey, I haven't seen Fred around. Where is he, anyway?" And the reply may come back, "What? Haven't you heard? Fred is dead and buried!" That's our way of saying, "He's really gone!" When a person has been buried, that person has become pure past, only memory. As Karl Barth says in *Credo,* we see, in the death of Jesus, "a self-surrender of God to the fate and state of man." He is crucified, dead, and buried! In the mention of Pontius Pilate, we remember how Jesus was delivered by him to the soldiers and was crucified, dead, and buried. We remember how his enemies came to taunt him and the women came to mourn him, when he was crucified, dead, and buried. And how Joseph of Arimathea begged his body from Pilate and offered his family tomb so that the crucified Jesus now dead could be buried. And he was! They wrapped him in a linen shroud, laid him in a hewn rock tomb, and rolled a great stone over the mouth of that sepulcher. Hear the noise as they knock loose the wedge and that wheel of rock rolls down its track across the opening to seal the body of Jesus forever from the sunlight. Or so they thought. He was crucified, dead, and buried.

Descended into Hell

What a place to end the chapter! This phrase is among the most difficult of all the phrases in the Creed for most people to understand. It does not mean, and there is no sense in which it could mean, that he descended into hell to suffer for his sins. Something else entirely is intended. I could turn to historical scholarship and say that this is a late fourth-century addition to the Creed, which it is, but that doesn't help much. Why was it added? Not just to go one step further in saying that he died. Let me propose two ideas. First, hell has only one central meaning in scripture. It is the place, or better yet the condition, of separation from God. Therefore, it symbolizes isolation, utter aloneness, the great divorce from the all-pervasive love of the Father. It seems to me this is what Jesus was feeling in what theologians call "the cry of dereliction" from the cross, "My God, my God, why hast thou forsaken me?" (Matt. 27:46). Jesus descended into hell when he carried the sin of the world. His unity with the Father was hidden in that awful darkness. We see here, as in no other place, Jesus' humanness. He enters the abyss of death utterly rejected and forsaken by all, and the oppression is so great that he can no longer see the face of God.

Second, since Jesus descended into hell, there is no place closed to him forever. There is no night so dark, there is no depression so deep, there is no failure so abysmal, there is no sorrow so heavy, there is no hell so distant from God that the Savior cannot find me and rescue me from whatever power of chaos, selfishness, hell, or despair would hide from me the loving face of the Father. He will redeem me from darkness and present me forgiven, reclaimed for life and love.

Though we talk about the death of Jesus and the descent into hell, we also know what comes next, that this is not the final word. "He suffered under Pontius Pilate, was crucified, dead, and buried; he descended into hell." But there was more to come.

Questions for Reflection

1. Explore your comprehension of the phrase, "Jesus died for me."

2. Jesus gave up his life for us. What is the place of self-denial in Christian discipleship?

3. Does a follower of Jesus Christ suffer in this world? Do you suffer as a follower of Christ? How?

4. When has Christ's suffering for you changed your action toward others?

5. What makes love redemptive, or restorative, for others?

6

The Third Day He Rose Again from the Dead . . .

The Apostles' Creed is a bare-bones statement of Christian essentials. Here, packed into 110 words, is the core of Christian belief in a creed whose beginnings trace back to the first century A.D. If we were to distill the essence of the Creed even more, we would discover words like these: "Jesus died for us and is risen." This is the critical center on which every other statement rests. All else moves toward it or takes its meaning from it. Chapter 5 spoke to the first half, "was crucified, dead, and buried," and this chapter speaks to the second half, "the third day he rose again from the dead." This is the irreducible core of the gospel.

Let me draw a couple of analogies. The essence of American democracy is freedom and justice for all. These great realities lie at the heart of the American dream. You may differ on peripheral issues such as economic philosophy, the balance of state and federal powers, the strength of the presidency, but unless the core holds firm, nothing will hang together. Freedom and justice for all is the essence of the nation. As a second analogy, in the education of our children, the core is the ability to read. You may differ on what subjects to include in the curriculum—computer science, sex education, Russian studies—but you have to be clear that reading is fundamental to learning. Unless the core remains firm, the educational process will fail.

I think you see where I am going. What freedom and justice are to democracy, what reading is to learning, the resurrection of Jesus is to Christianity. If this faith of ours is to be cohesive, if it is to have validity and life, then the center must be firm, "the third day he rose again from the dead." Using this phrase from the Creed, I want to discuss two points: Easter fact and Easter faith.

Easter Fact

Christianity is a historical faith, anchored as it is to actual times and places. We are not talking about Zeus holding council on Mount Olympus or about Odin's hall of slain warriors in Valhalla. These are mythological figures and places. We are talking about first-century Israel under the rule of Rome, where Pontius Pilate, prefect of Judea, delivered Jesus to soldiers of the Tenth Roman Legion to be scourged and crucified. We are saying that Judas betrayed him, Peter denied him, and all the rest fled when he was arrested and tried. We are saying that a rich citizen of Jerusalem named Joseph gave his own stone tomb for the burial, that they laid him there on Friday and sealed the tomb with a great rock. Then, though the Romans posted a guard, though Jesus was wrapped in a linen shroud and laid on a rock shelf, though the disciples had given up hope and retreated in fear behind closed doors, the tomb was empty when the sun came up on Sunday. You can try to explain it away. The disicples stole the body, or Jesus revived and walked out, or the early church fabricated the story, but these hollow explanations are contradicted by the Easter story and by the explosive rise of the early church. Paul mentioned people who experienced Jesus alive after that first Easter; he wrote about it twenty years after the events, as if to say to a rising generation, "If you doubt it, go and talk to them. Many are still living" (see 1 Cor. 15:3–8).

To tell the Easter story simply as historical fact is to stop far short of what must be said and, in fact, of what the New Testament itself says. If this is historical, if this is an event in time and space as the death of Julius Caesar is an event in time and space, then it is just about the most sensational event in time and space that we might imagine, comparable, at least, to the touching down on earth of spaceships and space beings from another world. Yet, the New Testament says, "We know that Christ being raised from the dead will never die again; death no longer has dominion over him" (Rom. 6:9). Hey! That's news! But how is the church to handle it? With headlines? With trumpets and cannons? Since we have a story like no other story, shall we push it, publicize it, promote it?

Well, no, not really, at least not in the style of the advertising world. One has to ask, How do people respond to sensational news? How do they react to seemingly incredible news of which they have no firsthand information or personal experience? They don't respond well. There are those who swear on a stack of Bibles that they have been on board a spacecraft. Call me a skeptic if you will, an unbeliever, but until one of those football-field-sized objects with the green lights lands in my backyard, I will continue to smile and say, "Sure, you've been on board!"

This is the way the disciples reacted to the women who came breathless with news of a risen Jesus. Luke recorded their unbelief, "But these words seemed to them an idle tale, and they did not believe them" (24:11; see also vv. 1–10).

Recall with me another story from Luke (16:19–31). There was a rich man who lived in the lap of luxury. At his gate lay a beggar namd Lazarus ill and in need. The rich man paid him no attention. Both men died, the poor man finding a place in heaven, the rich man finding a place in hell. It was the plea of the rich man, tormented man, that father Abraham send a special messenger to his five brothers, lest they come to the same place. "Send Lazarus to warn them," begged the rich man. Abraham replied, "They have Moses and the prophets; let your brothers hear them." But the rich man replied, "If someone goes to them from the dead, they will repent." "No," said Abraham, "they will not be convinced, even if someone should rise from the dead."

Who is right? Wouldn't we, many of us, side with the rich man and not with Abraham? Surely, if someone were to rise from the dead, then that would be the end of doubt and the beginning of faith! This is the belief that if we could prove it, submit it to analysis, then the door to faith would open. And that's a tempting assumption in a scientific age. If we could just get to Easter's empty tomb with our calipers and camera, a couple of first-rate glossy photos, the sworn testimony of a Roman guard, boy, that would do it! We would soon convince the world about the validity of Easter.

Obviously, this will not work. The truth of the resurrection rests on more than physical evidence and is bigger than historical event. Fact, yes, but how strange a fact, how unusual its telling. We are in history, but it is as if another reality beyond history is breaking in. How hard, if not impossible, to harmonize the Gospel accounts of the resurrection appearances. They are like flashes of light, like the parting of an invisible curtain that lets in glimpses of the glory of another world. Jesus appears in Jerusalem, then he is ninety miles away in Galilee. He is absent, then he is present inside locked doors where disciples have gathered, and he says to their troubled hearts, "Peace be with you" (John 20:21). Doubting Thomas reaches out a hesitating finger and touches nailprints—yes, it is Jesus indeed, crucified but alive. Jesus lights a fire on the shore of the Lake of Galilee, broils a breakfast of fish and, looking into Peter's eyes, says, "Do you love me?" (John 21:4–17). What stories these, what wonder present! Do we have eyes to see, we denizens of this age of technology? Surely, there is more to this world of ours, and these questing spirits of ours, than what we can see with our physical eyes and touch with our fingers.

Easter Faith

Now we come to the second point about this phrase from the Creed. If one strand of the Easter truth is an empty tomb, anchoring the Easter witness to history, then the other strand is a risen, living Christ. As I have been saying, that is in the realm of fact but much more. That Jesus is alive again is Christianity's center, and as such Easter is ultimately mysterious, permanently and perpetually provocative.

The disciples did not prepare a list of arguments for the empty tomb. Peter did not carry in his briefcase the linen shroud in which the body had been wrapped. This was not the nature of their witness. Instead, they went everywhere proclaiming, "He is alive, we have met him, death is defeated, he is the Christ, there is a new world!"

Easter, then, is more than evidence of an empty tomb. It is an experience of presence, the presence of a risen, living Christ. At dawn Mary is in Joseph's garden, weeping because she believes the body of Jesus has been stolen. There is a figure in the garden, and scarcely seeing him through her tears, Mary thinks he is the gardener. "Sir," she says, "if you have carried him away, tell me where you have laid him." Only when he speaks does she recognize him, only when he calls her name, "Mary," does she know him (John 20:15–16). It is an experience of presence.

Two disciples are on the road to Emmaus when a stranger meets them and walks with them. He asks them what they are taking about, and they say, "Don't you know? Jesus of Nazareth, a prophet mighty in deed and word before God and all the people, has been put to death in Jerusalem. We had hoped he was the one to redeem Israel" (Luke 24:13–21, AP). At the end of the journey they invite him into their home for the evening meal. He takes bread in his hands, blesses and breaks it, and in the breaking of the bread, they recognize him. Then he is gone, vanished from their sight. They say, "Did not our hearts burn within us while he talked to us on the road, while he opened to us the scriptures?" (Luke 24:28–32). That is Easter faith, the heart made open for the presence of Christ, and it is an experience of presence.

Nor has this changed in our own day. Indeed, there has never been a generation when Christianity has not been a faith that is passed from life to life, as one candle is lighted from another. Those of us for whom Jesus is alive keep saying to those around us, in one way or another, "He is alive, we have met him, death is defeated, he is the Christ, there is a new world."

As long as Easter is merely a great ecclesiastical

holiday proclaiming astonishing news, it will remain unconvincing and will lack the power to claim us as disciples and make us Easter people. Only when we see Easter as the celebration that Jesus is alive for us will we comprehend why there are trumpets and lilies and joy.

"The third day he rose from the dead." There is a depth in this sentence that goes beyond our personal experience of Christ. It is a gloriously personal truth, but that does not exhaust its meaning. If Jesus has burst open the iron gates of death which have kept us captive from the beginning, if one man, fully human, is not subject to death's irreversible dominion, then there is, indeed, a new world. Here is a truth with cosmic significance. Death, hell, darkness, and despair are defeated, and the future is broken open for the limitless possibilities of the sons and daughters of God. Here is finality! When Jesus rises from his tomb, death is mortally wounded. He has experienced death triumphantly and is *Christus Victor,* Christ the Conqueror. That is why we Christians say, "Life and not death, light and not darkness, love and not despair, these are the great realities."

In the Eastern Orthodox celebration, there is a service in the sanctuary on Saturday night before Easter. People come into a very dimly lighted church. There is a closed coffin in the front. All the icons are draped in black; no candle burns. Somber scriptures are read of Jesus' suffering, crucifixion, and burial. The atmosphere is heavy with darkness and death. At midnight the priests lights one candle, and from it, the candle of each worshiper is lighted. They leave the sanctuary in silence and walk three times around the block in a single-file, candle-lighted procession. It is a long walk. When they return, the sanctuary has been transformed. The coffin is empty and open, the icons are uncovered, Easter lilies are everywhere, and the worship place is ablaze with light. As the people come in and stand in the rear, the priest rises and cries out, "Christ is risen!" And with one voice, the people respond, the sound filling the sanctuary and echoing from the walls, "He is risen indeed!"

And what of us? What is our response to the New Testament witness? What message do we hear, what is the nature of our affirmation when we say, "The third day he rose again from the dead"?

Questions for Reflection

1. Why does this chapter say that the resurrection belongs to the irreducible core of the gospel?

2. What distinguishing marks can you recognize in a person, or a congregation, for whom Easter is an experience of the presence of Christ?

3. Is it true that seeing is believing?

4. Is the meaning of the resurrection felt in Christian funerals you have attended?

5. Discuss the incident in which the risen Christ asks Peter, "Do you love me?" Where does love for Christ lead?

---·**7**·---

He Ascended into Heaven, and Sitteth at the Right Hand of God the Father Almighty . . .

These words are about the power and authority of "Jesus Christ his only son our Lord." In order to move into the meaning of this creedal statement, let's think about our experience of power in our growing-up years. It's really a question of what melody we hear. We learned one melody when we watched our parents compete for family leadership. There was Dad, blustering and overt perhaps; there was Mom, quiet, more subtle perhaps, but playing the same game. Maybe in your family the roles were reversed or different. Each parent had a point of view, each wanted to exercise authority in the family.

This melody was reinforced in school and among our friends, as we learned how to gain the competitive edge and to press our advantage. Follow the leaders, avoid the losers, be number one. We adopted this as our song, and some of it was necessary.

When we grew up, we hummed this melody as we raised our children, as we earned our living, as we made our friendships and pursued our leisure. This melody is called "the love of power."

There is another melody. We learned this one from our parents too, to the extent that we saw their love for each other and felt their warm response to us. This was not an easy melody to whistle in school or among our friends. Indeed, we saw a lot of cruelty, and there were few times when someone gave up an advantage for someone else or welcomed someone who was odd or handicapped or unattractive.

Even today, in the places where we work, or in the circles in which we move, the situation hasn't changed much. Seldom are the disadvantaged given a hand up, seldom are the poor, the isolated, or the ugly welcomed among the affluent, the accepted, and the beautiful. When they are, it is rare and, therefore, remarkable. We call this melody, faint as it may be, "the power of love." The quality of your life depends on which melody you hear and heed, whether for you the love of power or the power of love is central.[1]

In this chapter on the Apostles' Creed, the theme is the ascension, a theme inseparable from the power of Christ. Here we no longer speak of a crucified Christ, with a face marred more than any man's (see Isa. 53), but a risen Christ with a face "like the sun shining in full strength" (Rev. 1:16), ascended and sitting on the right hand of the Majesty on high (Matt. 26:64, AP). He is, therefore, a Christ of unimaginable power and dominion, who says from the far side of death, "all authority in heaven and on earth has been given to me" (Matt. 28:18). He is the one to whom God has given "the name which is above every name, that at the name of Jesus every knee should bow, . . . and every tongue confess that Jesus Christ is Lord, to the glory of God the Father" (Phil. 2:9–11). The reason that he is the Lord is not the love of power, and the right to rule that power gives, but rather the power of love. This majestic Christ, this conquering Christ, this cosmic Christ, still bears the name, "Jesus" and carries in his hands the print of the nails. He has given himself for us in sacrificial love, in spite of all our brokenness and rebellion, and God has vindicated that sacrifice in the resurrection. At the heart of our universe is not unreasoning chance, not the love of power, but the power of love.

In this chapter we are considering the power of Christ in this creedal statement, "he ascended into heaven, and sitteth at the right hand of God the Father Almighty." Here are three ideas to lead us through these ancient words: the mystery, the mood, and the meaning of the ascension.

The Mystery

I have stood on Olivet in Jerusalem, on the Mount of Ascension, and thought about this sentence: "As they were looking on, he was lifted up, and a cloud took him out of their sight" (Acts 1:9). That's not an easy verse to hear or to accept. What do we do with it? I know. Put it right up there on the shelf marked "Ancient Mythologies." Or we could define the ascension as "physical displacement in a direction perpendicular to the horizon of Jerusalem."[2]

Why these criticisms and doubts about the New Testament account? Because we "moderns" see that the first-century world believed in a three-story universe: heaven above, earth beneath, hell beneath the earth. There it is in Luke's words, "While he blessed them, he parted from them, and was carried up into heaven" (24:51).

Obviously, people say, this story was written to fit the cosmology of the day and can bear no resemblance to truth or actual event. To say that, it seems to me, is to make a light-headed analysis of what is being said in the ascension stories. It reminds me of the comment a man made about an acquaintance, "Way down deep he's a very shallow person." Well, way down deep this is a very shallow analysis. There were things happening in the disciples' experience of Jesus for which they had no adequate words. They were always stretching to find ways to say what they wanted to say and were unable to capture it. The experience was too big for the words. Listen to John, for instance, "We beheld his glory, the glory as of the only begotten of the Father, full of grace and truth" (John 1:14, KJV). Now that's not bad, but you can hear John straining to capture within the boundaries of language a Person whose boundaries are limitless. The same is true of the resurrection stories, which we have considered already. "He is risen!" These words of indescribable joy, of undeniable discovery, are on the lips of the disciples. The stories, however, remain only glorious shadows of the reality behind them. The same is true of the ascension.

Look at it this way. The ascension is the last of the postresurrection appearances of Jesus. It is very like the others because of his sudden appearance and departure. He had to leave sometime and in some way, and it is important to the disciples to know that he is returning to the Father. Otherwise they would be forever wondering, "What happened to him. Where is he?"

It is obvious, is it not, if one looks beneath the surface of the text, that the disciples were not so naive as to think he had simply gone to some locale "perpendicular to the horizon." They understood that ascension meant dominion, power, majesty, that it was stepping through an invisible door into the glory of the kingdom of God. They sensed, but did not grasp the reality behind the image of the ascension. That is why "they returned to

Jerusalem with great joy, and were continually in the temple blessing God" (Luke 24:52–53). The reason for their joy was that they had met Jesus, beyond a shadow of a doubt, and understood that he was the Christ, the God-sent Christ vindicated in the resurrection, who now was joined in love and power with the Father.

The Mood

Luke recorded that the risen Christ appeared to the eleven disciples. He said to them, "Why are you troubled?" (24:38). Then he showed them the marks of the crucifixion, so there could be no mistaking who he was. "Touch me," he said. That is, "Put your hands on me and be certain. No spirit has physical presence like this. It's really me!" What a wonderful phrase Luke added, how real and believable, "While they still disbelieved for joy, and wondered, he said to them, 'Have you anything here to eat?' They gave him a piece of broiled fish, and he took it and ate before them" (24:41–43, AP).

Luke noted, "Then he opened their minds to understand the scriptures" (24:45). Jesus said, "It is written, that the Christ should suffer and on the third day rise from the dead, and that repentance and forgiveness of sins should be preached in his name to all nations. . . . You are witnesses of these things" (Luke 24:46–48). He commissioned them to cover the earth with his name.

He led them out to a place near Bethany, and as his final action for his beloved disciples, he lifted up his hands and blessed them. In the act of the blessing, he was taken from them. Whatever the method of his leaving, whatever the disciples saw, whatever that final parting, they knew they would never lose him. "I am with you till the end of time" (Matt. 28:20, AP) was burned into their minds and branded on their spirits. That is why they returned to Jerusalem with great joy. The mood of the ascension is not a mood of grief or sadness in departing—it is a mood of love, of blessing, of confidence, and of irrepressible joy. They returned to Jerusalem in the greatest expectation, awaiting the promised power, the visitation of the Spirit of Jesus, the event that gave the church its birth, which we know as Pentecost.

What is the mood of the church today? Do we in our various congregations know ourselves to be the community of Jesus, as did the disciples? Can we sense his hands stretched over us in blessing? Does his risen life leave upon us the indelible mark of joy? Do we live in the power of his Spirit, expecting that the fruit of the gospel will grow and ripen in our midst? And, therefore, do we know what we mean when we say, "Jesus Christ is Lord"? It is all there in the account of the ascension.

The Meaning

First of all, let me note that the ascension is not a minor doctrine. It is inseparable from the resurrection and completes its meaning. Yes, Jesus is risen, but to what purpose? The New Testament makes clear that he is risen to be the Lord, to exercise authority, to be the head of the church:

> God exalted him at his right hand as Leader and Savior.
> —Acts 5:31

> Christ Jesus, who died, yes, who was raised from the dead, who is at the right hand of God, who indeed intercedes for us.
> —Romans 8:34

> If then you have been raised with Christ, seek the things that are above, where Christ is, seated at the right hand of God.
>
> —Colossians 3:1

> Looking to Jesus the pioneer and perfecter of our faith, who for the joy that was set before him endured the cross, despising the shame, and is seated at the right hand of the throne of God.
>
> —Hebrews 12:2

> [He] has gone into heaven and is at the right hand of God, with angels, authorities, and powers subject to him.
>
> —1 Peter 3:22

The formulaic expression, "sitteth at the right hand of God," simply means that he is in the central place of authority, power, and acceptance with God.

Here we leave the past tense in the Creed and come into the present tense. "Conceived by the Holy Ghost, born of the Virgin Mary, suffered under Pontius Pilate, was crucified, dead, and buried . . . descended into hell; the third day he rose from the dead; he ascended into heaven"—all of this is in the past tense. But now we hear the present tense for the first time, "and sitteth at the right hand of God the Father Almighty." Christians believe this and confess it in the Creed. It means that Jesus is Lord. It means that his Spirit is present, his power available, his love apprehensible, his truth pervasive, and his rule extends over time, and death. He is Lord. And one day the kingdoms of this world, and all the worlds that are, will be brought into glorious harmony with his loving purpose. What is the meaning of the ascension? That Jesus is Lord.

And what else? That Jesus is near. Leslie Weatherhead put it this way, "The Ascension does not mean that He passed to some distant heaven beyond those possibilities of friendship, but that He widened the possibilities so that for all [people] He is the ever-available."[3] That is the meaning of the ascension, and Pentecost to follow, that Christ is among us in love and power, available to our weakness, and our strengthening for his purposes. His promise is for the church across the generations, "Where two or three are gathered in my name, there am I in the midst of them" (Matt. 18:20). What is the meaning of the ascension? That Jesus is near.

And what else? That Jesus is the head of the church, which is his body. The ascension, you see, is the beginning, not the ending. It is proper that the account of the ascension stands first in Acts, which probably should be called, "The Book of the Acts of the Early Church." Jesus ascended. Not many days later the Spirit descended, and the church was born.

We are living, then, in an interim period, a period between the ascension and the return of Christ. We are living in the age of the church. It is an age of grace and an age of the Spirit in which we have, by God's mercy and love, opportunity to proclaim to the world the good news about Jesus Christ. What did he say? "This gospel of the kingdom will be preached throughout the whole world, as a testimony to all nations; and then the end will come" (Matt. 24:14). What a privilege, then, and what a high commission, to bear witness to God's love and power while we have time, human time. What is the meaning of the ascension? That Jesus is the head of the church.

And what else? Jesus ascended, or if you will, he stepped through that invisible curtain into the land of light we say is God's kingdom. Therefore, we have that same future as our heritage. Jesus said, "Because I live, you will live also" (John 14:19), and "I go to prepare a place for you" (John 14:2). Paul told the same truth: "For if we have been united with him in a death like his [through baptism], we shall certainly be united with him in a resurrection like his" (Rom. 6:5). What is the meaning of the ascension? That our final end is a land of light, a timeless dimension that Jesus called "the kingdom."

"He ascended into heaven, and sitteth at the right hand of God the Father Almighty." These words are but shadows of the vast reality that lies behind them. By faith, and because of Christ, that reality is our homeland.

Questions for Reflection

1. "He ascended into heaven." Does this have spatial meanings?

2. What is the nature of Christ's power?

3. How is this power evident in your life?

4. Is the ascension celebrated in your church in the sense of the contemporary and ever present Christ?

5. How is the mission of the church dependent on the ascension of Christ?

8

From Thence He Shall Come to Judge the Quick and the Dead . . .

As you drive north on Route 82, between Montgomery and Tuscaloosa, Alabama, you will see a large sign spangled with blue stars, unless the termites have gotten it by now. It stands out over the surrounding landscape, planted on the top of an eroded hillside, declaring its message to passing sinners. Large, blood-red letters, having withstood the bleaching effects of the the southern sun, puzzle and threaten the uninitiated with the message: Watch—King Jesus Is Coming Soon!

In the small town of Grannis, Arkansas, a few years ago, twenty-five people kept vigil in a small house awaiting the second coming of Jesus and the end of the world. Neighbors reported a lot of screaming going on and the sight of members dressed in white ascension robes. Sheriff A. L. Hadaway took custody of six children who were living there. "We don't have any special plans for this Christmas," said one of the group members, "because we won't be here." But Christmas passed without apocalypse, and the fervor of the group waned.

And, lest you think I'm picking on the South, let's talk about Boston. William Miller lectured there in the fall of 1844, and the whole city was in a tizzy. He said that Jesus would return that October 22 and would destroy his enemies. When October 22 came and went without event, Miller was somewhat chagrined, and the citizens of Boston were disenchanted with dating Jesus' return. [1]

As you can tell by these examples, the Apostles' Creed has brought us to a subject that can certainly qualify as sensational, the return of Jesus or, as the particular friends of this return call it, the second coming of Christ. I will use a verse of scripture from the Book of Revelation as a catalyst for the discussion of this theme. (Another name for Revelation, by the way, is the Apocalypse, which means "the unveiling.") "[Jesus] who testifies to these things says, 'Surely I am coming soon.' Amen. Come, Lord Jesus!" (Rev. 22:20). From that verse come these three ideas: the Day of Doom, the Day of the Lord, and the Day of Judgment. So, fasten your safety belts, and away we go.

The Day of Doom, or Doomsday

Many people, millions of them, see the return of Christ as an event of destruction far beyond anything the world has ever known. These people spend time exploring the Book of Revelation in minute detail. Have you read it lately? Wow! Demonic spirits loosed on the earth when the bottomless pit that holds Satan is opened; seven great bowls of wrath poured out; three great calamities pronounced with the words, "Woe, woe, woe, to those who dwell on the earth" (8:13); hailstones as big as basketballs; the beast with ten horns, part leopard, part bear, part lion, rising from the sea; the dragon and his evil angels fighting against Michael, the captain of the hosts of God; blood on earth as high as horses' bridles; fire, flood, famine, and disaster—these four horsemen of the Apocalypse gallop across its pages. I can remember, as a high-school student, reading this book at a sitting and being utterly spellbound. This language reaches us at level below the rational mind, speaking to unconscious impulses within us. Its symbolism, its profound mythology, its primal images, and its enormous struggle between good and evil are almost hypnotic.

It was written, scholars tell us, in the midst of persecution. Everywhere Christians were being put to death by cross, by sword, by fire, by wild beasts in the Coliseum. What is the great Babylon, Babylon the mighty, the harlot, the beast, the dragon? It is Rome, which with deadly force was destroying the people of God.

At a deeper level, Babylon is the pervasive evil we can trace across all our history—destructive force, chaotic power, evil purpose, greed, these things war against the world. The forces of love, of civilization, of peace and friendship, of gentleness and mercy are besieged and beaten down so that millions suffer. The Book of Revelation is right. There is a darkness in the world, far beyond our ability to define or comprehend, a darkness always shrouded in mystery. One does not have to search far for examples—the Thirty Years' War that decimated the population of Europe, World War II with its genocide and terror, the irrational evil we see happening in our world on a daily basis—these things can convince us that the plagues of Revelation have been happening all along. The Day of Doom is a familiar day in our history.

It has come to my attention that some of my

Christian brothers and sisters are not the only ones prophesying doomsday. An article in *New Republic* recalls a 1970 *Life* magazine article which reported that

> there was a probability that by 1980 urban dwellers would have to wear gas masks to breathe, by the early 1980s a smog inversion would kill thousands of people in a major city, and by 1985 the amount of sunlight reaching the earth would be reduced by half and new diseases that man could not resist would reach plague proportions.[2]

There are economic doomsday schools that want us to convert all our money to gold, population doomsday schools predicting that by the year 2020 each human being will have one square foot of earth on which to live, and nuclear doomsday schools saying we won't make it out of the 1980s. I hope the peace movement, which I strongly affirm, will exercise a wise and passionate political pressure toward a mutual reduction in nuclear arms and will not spend too much time drawing pictures of apocalypse.

Doomsday talk is a mentality. Watch the hype of the doomsayers, the exaggeration, which often seems to obscure truth rather than reveal it. Doomsday talk polarizes, paralyzes, sensationalizes. It is pretty good at the seduction and manipulation of people. It distorts and confuses; it makes the uninformed and unthinking depend on the highly questionable interpretations of the so-called experts. That is why doomsday schools become a haven for the lunatic fringe, the hucksters, the money-grubbers, and the power hungry. Keep a wary eye on those who keep saying, "The sky is falling." It goes without saying, I hope, that there are many real dangers on which we all must keep our steady, level gaze and be prepared to take positive action.

So, this is the end of the first point. I have begun by talking about doomsday because I want to acknowledge that there is a lot of craziness attached to this whole subject of Jesus' return. That does not mean we simply steer clear of what appears to be a rather major piece of biblical teaching.

The Day of the Lord

"This may hurt the cemetery business," said a smiling preacher on a recent television program, "but I don't own a plot." The faithful hardly needed to be told why, but for the benefit of those who hadn't heard, he explained that he, like others who were "saved," was going not down into the grave but up into the clouds to meet the returning Christ at his second coming, which would surely occur in a brief span of time.

If you don't think a lot of people are caught up in this belief and look for an imminent return of Christ within this present generation, then you aren't reading Hal Lindsey. His book, *The Late Great Planet Earth,* went through twenty-one printings in the first twenty-six months. A subculture supporting these publications is vast and committed, numbering in the millions.[3]

There will be (this is a safe prediction) an increasing fervor about Jesus' return during the rest of this century. Why? Because the magical year 2000 is approaching. Like a great magnet, that millennial year will attract mounting belief in the end of the world. If you have followed the teaching of those who are busy charting the end of the world, then 2000 is a good time for the end of time as we know it and the beginning of the millennium, a one thousand-year rule of peace before the kingdom of God comes in its fullness. Some teach that for the seven and a half years before the millennium there will be a time of terror such as the human race has never witnessed! All the plagues of Revelation will be poured out on the earth. But they won't affect true believers in Jesus, because believers will be caught up in the air to meet the returning Christ before the tribulation begins. There are those who draw charts depicting how all these things will happen. For instance, Brother McKeever writes a book on the tribulation and how to prepare for it. There is a chapter, "Preparing for Supernatural Warfare."[4] It puts one in mind of the War Scroll, which was part of the Dead Sea Scrolls, a document drawing up battle plans for joining God's angels in the war against Rome's legions.

If you are not an initiate in these matters, all of this will make your head swim. Let me, then, do some simple teaching about the return of Jesus. That he will come again is central to the New Testament witness. Three hundred verses talk about it in one way or another; that's one out of every thirteen verses in the New Testament so it must be important. Here are Jesus' words in John 14:3: "I will come again and will take you to myself." Sometimes it is called his "appearing," as in Titus 2:13, "Awaiting our blessed hope, the appearing of the glory of our great God and Savior Jesus Christ." Sometimes just "the coming," as in "May your spirit and soul and body be kept sound and blameless at the coming of our Lord Jesus Christ" (1 Thess. 5:23). Sometimes it is called "the day of the Lord," for example, "The day of the Lord will come like a thief in the night" (1 Thess. 5:2). First Corinthians refers to the Christian as waiting "for the revealing of our Lord Jesus Christ" (1:7). Or, as the Apostles' Creed puts it, "from thence he shall come to judge the quick and the dead." From thence? What is that? From his ascension to the right hand of God, from his position of power and authority as Lord of the world.

Okay, we accept as biblically central that Christ will come again, but what does it mean? *First, it means mystery!* "He is coming with the clouds," says Revelation 1:7. Clouds are the biblical symbol of mystery and of the presence of God. "Lo, I am coming to you in a thick cloud," said God to Moses at mount Sinai (Exod. 19:9; see also 24:15ff.). A cloud, symbolizing the divine presence, covered the tabernacle in the wilderness (Exod. 40:34–36). A cloud shrouded the mercy seat of the ark of the covenant, the place where the presence of God dwelt (Lev. 16:2). A cloud of glory, the very majesty of God, filled the temple of Solomon at its dedication (1 Kings 8:10–11). When the New Testament says that Jesus is coming with the clouds, it is a powerful symbol of mystery and divinity.

It follows then that attempts to date the coming, to draw charts of the last days, to busy ourselves sketching in the contours of heaven, are inconsistent with the mystery of the coming so central to scripture. Obviously, it is an event beyond our human power to describe, date, or classify. Jesus himself said, "Of that day and hour no one knows, not even the angels of heaven, nor the Son, but the Father only" (Matt. 24:36).

Second, it means purpose and destiny! Not limitless cycles of human history going nowhere, not a lost world adrift in the ocean of space, this is not the final meaning. There is, rather, "a divinity that shapes our ends."[5] There is a God who is working out a divine purpose as year succeeds to year.[6] Just as the resurrection is the foundation upon which our faith rests, so the return of Christ is the horizon toward which we move and on which we fix our hope of the life eternal. One day, a day lost in mystery but visible to the eye of faith, God will draw the final curtain on the human drama, and time will be no more. By the way, for all the preoccupation of those who draw charts of the last days, they do live in passionate hopefulness, longing for the appearing of our Lord Jesus Christ. Perhaps they feel, more than most of us who are Christian, a burning desire for the completion of all things, for the time when "the earth shall be full of the glory of God as the waters cover the sea."[7] That passionate longing for fulfillment, for the day of the Lord, is a fire of expectation in the New Testament, indeed in the whole Bible. You can hear it in Revelation 22:20, at the very end of the Bible, where Jesus says, "Surely I am coming soon," and where the church makes its glad response, "Amen. Come, Lord Jesus!" Paul spoke of this new age in Romans 8:22; he envisioned the whole creation groaning with birth pangs, awaiting its deliverance. Just beyond the rim of the horizon, just beyond the reach of our minds, we sense the kingdom, the day of the Lord, which means the transformation of all things. Deep within us, woven into our native impulses, is the dream of a golden tomorrow. "Beloved," said John, "we are God's children now; it does not yet appear what we shall be, but we know that when he appears we shall be like him, for we shall see him as he is" (1 John 3:2).

On top of Riverside Church in New York City stands the angel Gabriel. He is poised, expectant, gazing upward, horn in hand, waiting eagerly to sound the last trumpet call to welcome the returning Christ. Like him, we Christians live in hope. This is God's world. That Christ will return is the assurance that God is sovereign over the whole creation, that God's purposes flow from the work of Jesus Christ, who is the Lord of all. We do not know when the end shall be or how it shall come, but come it shall, and we are ready for the dawn, the day of the Lord.

The Day of Judgment

If I had a nickel for every story a parishioner has told me about Saint Peter and the pearly gates, and about who gets in and who doesn't, I could take a trip to China. These are essentially stories about the judgment. The Creed says that "he [Jesus] shall come to judge the quick and the dead." That latter phrase does not refer to traffic in your hometown where if you're not quick, you're dead. *Quick* means "living."

The medieval church spent a lot of time and energy drawing landscapes of hell. Tapestries, sculptures, paintings, and frescoes vividly portrayed the terrors of the judgment. The Italian poet, Dante, wrote an epic poem, *The Divine Comedy,* which includes a section "The Inferno" in which there is a famous inscription over the gates of hell, "Abandon all hope, you who enter."

Today we are not quite as busy making maps of hell or preaching hellfire and damnation sermons, though you may have heard them somewhere or even have been raised on them. Then what do we do with the biblical theme of judgment? Primarily, we Christians are always to look at judgment through the prism of the grace of our Lord Jesus Christ. The One who comes "to judge the quick and the dead" is the One who gave his life for us and pictured for us a waiting Father wanting to welcome us home no matter how far we have wandered. The Heidelberg Catechism puts it this way:

> *Question:* What comfort is it to thee that "Christ shall come again to judge the quick and the dead?"
>
> *Answer:* That in all my sorrows and persecutions, with uplifted head, I look for the very same person, who before offered Himself, for my

sake, to the tribunal of God, and hath re-
moved all curse from me.[8]

That we are mortal, that we are creatures of
conscience, moral beings by our very nature, these
things lead us to take the judgment seriously. Some
accounting will be required of us when we look into the
face of Christ. Yes, it matters whether I accept God's
love. Yes, it matters whether I love my neighbors or
exploit them. Yes, every day I frame a nature and a
character with which I shall cross the river of death. To
shape that character in the image of love, faith, and care
for neighbor is a rather critical factor. And yes, I fail,
repeatedly so, and almost no thought or action is
unmixed with selfishness. But I am secure since God's
love in Jesus Christ knows me at my worst and accepts
me anyway. Will we ever comprehend the freedom with
which God accepts us in Jesus Christ?

But the judgment is more than personal. It means that
God will restore order and banish chaos, that sorrow
and pain will be no more, that God's creation will be
healed, and that all which seeks to hurt, destroy, or war
against God will forever be vanquished. Until that time
we Christians are to carry Christ's love into our world
and to live in confidence. This is God's world, and God
is working out divine purposes, some of them through
us. "Amen. Come, Lord Jesus!"

Questions for Reflection

1. To what extent do you share in the New Testament anticipation of the return of Christ?

2. How do the bumper stickers announcing "Jesus Is Coming Soon" affect you?

3. Check the category which best describes your feelings about *judgment* and say why:
   a) never think about it _____
   b) makes me uneasy   _____
   c) seems unreal   _____
   d) motivates me to . . ._____

4. Do you think preoccupation with the return of Christ can separate us from service to Christ in this world?

5. Talk about a "doomsday mentality."

9

The Holy Ghost . . .

It's a normal Sunday morning in your church, and a visitor from another nation attends worship. A student at a nearby college, she is not a Christian. Having read about Christianity, she wants to know more. At the end of the service, she comes to the coffee hour, and when you introduce yourself, she has some questions for you: "I noticed that you have a curious theme running through your worship. You began with a strong processional hymn inviting God to join you, and I heard these words:

> Come, holy Comforter,
> Thy sacred witness bear,
> In this glad hour;
> Thou who almighty art,
> Now rule in every heart,
> And ne'er from us depart,
> Spirit of power![1]

"God the Creator—I know about that. Jesus—I know about him. But who, or what, is this Spirit of power? In the Apostles' Creed you confessed belief in 'the Holy Ghost.' Is this the same thing? Then when your pastor closed the service, he gave a blessing—it was called 'the benediction.' He said, 'The grace of our Lord Jesus Christ, the love of God, and the fellowship and communion of the Holy Spirit be with you all.' So, I believe in God, and I've heard about Jesus, but tell me, Christian church member, what does it mean when your church sings, talks, confesses, and gives blessings in the name of the Holy Spirit?"

How would you answer such a visitor? What do you know about the Holy Spirit? What part does the Spirit play in your understanding and experience of Christian faith? "Well," you say, "I'm a little foggy on that. Tell me, who is the Holy Spirit?" That is precisely the subject of this chapter on the Apostles' Creed. Let's explore the meaning of "the Holy Ghost."

The Place in the Creed

In the Creed are three articles of belief, or three major sections. The first article concerns God the Father: "I believe in God the Father Almighty, maker of heaven and earth." The second article concerns the Son: "And in Jesus Christ his only Son our Lord." Subpoints under the second article have to do with Jesus' birth, suffering, crucifixion, death, burial, descent into hell, resurrection, ascension, dominion, second coming, and judgment. This chapter begins the third article of the Creed with the words, "I believe in the Holy Ghost."

I have a couple of additional remarks to make on the way the Creed is constructed, drawing some insights from Karl Barth. This is the second time the word *credo* is used, *Credo in Spiritum Sanctum,* which is Latin for "I believe in the Holy Ghost." The first time *credo* was used, of course, was in the beginning, "I believe in God." This second use makes it emphatic. Read an exclamation point here, "I believe in the Holy Ghost!"

But why the exclamation? Because, for the first time, the individual Christian comes into the picture. What God in power and love has done in Jesus Christ has been done for each of us. Up to this point, there has been no indication of why God is doing all this. God is the Father Almighty, Jesus died and is risen, but to what end? What does it mean? How does it touch my life, if at all? This third article answers those questions. The items in this article—forgiveness, resurrection of the body, the life everlasting—no longer have the nature and activity of God for their main focus. The Creed now turns to the benefits for the believer, and it becomes intensely personal. *I* am the object of divine concern, *I* reap the result of God's work through Jesus. God loves *me,* and it is for *me* that these things have been accomplished and are made possible. As Karl Barth said, "We speak of the *Holy Spirit,* we speak of the Church, of forgiveness of sins, of the resurrection of the flesh and of eternal life, but just because and in so far as man gets a share in all that through the Holy Spirit."[2] To put it another way, in Jesus Christ we see the work of God objectively and externally; in the Holy Spirit we experience the work of God subjectively and internally.

One other comment on the place of the Holy Spirit in the Creed. Originally, I was going to alter the order of the subjects in this article of the Creed. "A little juggling of the subjects won't hurt," I speculated. It soon became apparent, however, as I began to study, that it wouldn't work. The Creed would not allow it. There is such a necessary progression, there is such a closely knit order, that one does violence to the Creed by rearranging the subject matter.

The Place in the Church

The church is the creation of the Holy Spirit. On Pentecost, in symbols of wind and fire, the Holy Spirit visited those early disciples waiting in an upper room in Jerusalem. Jesus had told them to wait for the promise of power from on high (Acts 1:8). Pentecost is the day on which the church was born. It was born, and is born, as we rest in the promise of Christ and wait for that promise to be fulfilled in our midst and in our being.

Sure, this sounds familiar and right. But is it more than theological language? Unless the language is the reflection of an experience that is in our bones, why should we bother? Is there a Holy Spirit? Who or what is he, or is it she, or it?

Open your mind for a minute. Put away the need for a spectrographic analysis of the Spirit, and exercise your faculty of imagination. Suppose we are, as I believe we are, created by God. By some incredibly long, complex process God has gathered together and ordered the atoms that compose these bodies of ours. Each atom, physicists tell us, is a universe held together by mysterious forces. Comparatively, there is as much space between the solid parts of the atom as there is between the planets and sun in our solar system. Carry your imagination another step. There is reason to believe that the energy holding together these bodies of ours is not just inside us but all around us and radiates from us. It is worth asking, as someone has suggested, whether we are in our bodies or our bodies are in us. Our human spirits are not really the products of our central nervous systems but products of this peculiar gathered energy. Sometimes we call it a "soul." That energy pattern, which is our very selves, is permeable by God's spirit if we allow our human spirits to be

92

receptive. That is why it was so critical for the disciples in the upper room to wait for the promise of "energy" from above—to be open, to be expectant, to be ready, to wait.

But what spirit is this? It is the Spirit of Jesus Christ. To be touched by the Holy Spirit is to be touched by Jesus, to be united with Jesus. When we say that "Jesus lives in the Christian's heart," we are saying that he abides with us, renewing who and what we are. We are no longer alone but are one with Christ in what theologians call a "mystical union." Our mortal nature is forever changed. As we make internal room, as we begin to unlock closed doors, that same Spirit begins within us a process of restoration. Most of the old wallpaper has to come down, the woodwork has to be sanded and finished, the fireplace set ablaze with love and gratitude, the halls and walls hung with new art, the stereo rewired for some new, glorious music. All the while the energy that is the essential self burns with a finer fire, finds a lovelier symmetry that in its nature is like the beauty of Christ. It is the work of the Spirit to form in us the image of Christ.

I am saying that the Holy Spirit is the Spirit of Christ. This is not to forget that first and foremost the Spirit is God's spirit, but to be faithful to the New Testament witness that reveals the Holy Spirit as inseparable from the person and work of Christ (see John 15:26; Acts 10:38; Rom. 8:9; Phil. 1:19). From Christ the Spirit comes, to him he leads, of him he makes us witnesses. The Spirit, however, comes to us not for our sakes alone, for some personal mystic subjectivity, but for witness. As we are formed in the likeness of Christ, it becomes the natural thing to direct our energies outward to others. We love because Christ first loved us. Having received, we give.

If you want a good definition of the place of the Spirit in the church, here is one by Martin Luther:

> The Holy Spirit has called me by the Gospel, enlightened me with his gifts and sanctified and preserved me in the true faith; even as he calls, gathers, enlightens and sanctifies the whole Christian Church on earth and preserves it in union with Jesus Christ in the one true faith.[3]

The Place in the Christian

I have not seen it, perhaps you have, but they tell me the cathedral at Chartres is a thing of beauty. One rides through flat, rural countryside and sees in the distance the twin towers of the great cathedral rising up out of the plain. It dominates the horizon. Some visitors, when they arrive and stand in the small square, are disappointed. The towers, the windows, and the entire structure seem drab, dull, a lifeless gray. From outside, the stained glass is almost mute.

But inside the cathedral, everything changes! The windows, the glorious windows of Chartres, are ablaze with color and light. They come to life, they speak, they tell their gospel story. And the great arches soar upward, drawing the eye and the soul to God. Outside is one thing, inside is another.

Something like that happens when people are touched by the Holy Spirit. The Christian faith, which before seemed little more than a mountain of religious words, suddenly is like an endless castle of light.

What is the place of the Holy Spirit in the Christian? An internal place, an enlivening place, a kindling place of light and color. The Spirit makes Jesus tangible and ushers us through a door of consciousness into a land Jesus called "the kingdom."

You may have noticed that my careful distinctions are breaking down. I cannot maintain a neat division between the place of the Spirit in the church and the place of the Spirit in the Christian. They keep running into each other, meeting each other, overlapping, interweaving. It is almost impossible to objectify the Spirit. Jesus said that the Spirit is like the wind, that while we can observe the effects, the essence is invisible to the human eye. And although we know the presence of the Spirit, and believe the New Testament witness that the Spirit gives the church its birth, we also know that the Spirit is not confined to the church or the believer's experience. The Spirit is, we remember, the life-force of God and, like wind, blows where God wills. The same Spirit who brooded over the chaos of Genesis 1 continues to brood over all that is not under God's gracious will.

Let me close the chapter by identifying three noticeable effects of the presence of the Spirit in the Christian. First are a perception of love internally and an expression of love externally. "God's love has been poured into our hearts through the Holy Spirit which has been given to us" (Rom. 5:5). The primary expression of the presence of the Holy Spirit is not in any particular gift. The primary expression of the Spirit's presence is an increasingly free, accepting, and glad-hearted love for other people, both inside and outside the Christian community. There are two distinctive definitions of God in the New Testament: "God is spirit" (John 4:24), and "God is love" (1 John 4:8).

Second is unity. This does not mean bland conformity or religious cliché. When Paul exhorted his churches to "maintain the unity of the Spirit in the bond of peace" (Eph. 4:3), he was talking about a common loyalty to Christ which never forgets we are part of one another, tied together by Christ's love. We are many, we are different, we are a collage of personalities and backgrounds, but like pieces of glass in a kaleidoscope, our lives fall together in patterns of beauty around Christ who is our center. In the words of a contemporary hymn, "We are one in the Spirit."

Third is hope. A lot of people go on hoping for things. They hope for a good health report, for a measure of prosperity, for friendship, for personal happiness, for notoriety, and for a host of other things. Christians, being bona fide members of the human race, hope for many of these things too, but there is an added ingredient. Christians, touched by the Spirit, go beyond hoping for things to a hope in life's center, Jesus Christ. Christians' deepest longings, ultimate sense of meaning, personal identity, rest in Jesus. All that Christians believe about the nature of the world, about human destiny, about the key to the mysteries, is tied to Jesus, the man for all seasons. Because of him, we are gripped by hope in the coming kingdom, in which we have already staked our claim by faith. The writer of Hebrews put it this way, "We have this [hope] as a sure and steadfast anchor of the soul" (6:19). These are some of the things the Creed means when it says, "I believe in the Holy Ghost."

Questions for Reflection

1. What about the Holy Spirit makes you the most uneasy?

2. What primary changes does the Holy Spirit bring about in the human heart?

3. Is the reality of God as three in one difficult for you to grasp? If so, how might you expand your understanding of the trinity?

4. For what reasons was the Holy Spirit given to the church?

5. How has the presence of the Holy Spirit been visible in churches you have known?

10

The Holy, Catholic Church . . .

We continue in the third section of the Apostles' Creed, the section on the Holy Spirit. The structure of the Creed, with its sections on God the Father, Jesus Christ, and the Holy Spirit, reflects the threefold baptismal command of Christ, "Go therefore and make disciples of all nations, baptizing them in the name of the Father and of the Son and of the Holy Spirit" (Matt. 28:19). By the early Middle Ages the Creed was used at baptisms throughout the Western church.[1]

This phrase is ninth in the series of twelve phrases which comprise the Creed. Why twelve? I could tell you it is because twelve is a great biblical number: the twelve apostles, who, early legend said, were its joint composers; the twelve tribes of Israel; the twelve cities of Benjamin; the twelve gates of the heavenly city; or the twelve fruits of the tree of life. But actually there are twelve segments because that's the way the subjects seemed to arrange themselves. So, with that gratuitous piece of honesty, here, for your consideration, instruction, inspiration, and love of the church of Jesus Christ, are three observations about the church: It is singled out, set apart, and sent forth.

Singled Out

The New Testament is written in Greek, and in that language the word we translate "church" is the word *ekklesia*. We get our word *ecclesiastical* from it. The root meaning of *ekklesia* is "called out." The church, then, is a company of people called out of their ordinary lives, out of the unbelieving world, for a particular undertaking, to carry God's Word and purpose in the world.

The Old Testament was translated into Greek some 2,300 years ago and was called "The Septuagint." Whenever, the Hebrew phrase, "people of God," appeared, it was translated with the word *ekklesia*. The point is that in both Old and New Testaments, there is a company of men and women singled out by God to be the agents of the divine purpose. Both in Israel and in Christ, God issues the call and makes the appeal, "I will be your God, and you will be my people" (see Gen. 17:7; Jer. 31:31–33; Rev. 21:3). That familiar sentence, formulaic sentence, is called "the covenant." Those who hear the call to be in covenant relationship with God must decide to accept or to refuse the offer. Those who say yes are the church.

This makes the church different from all other human communities. All the rest, all the other human communities I could list, are fashioned by human hope, need, and ingenuity. There is, for example, the family unit— mother, father, children. There is the larger family of the nation. There are racial and cultural families. There are contractual societies and unions, alliances, and fellowships. The Loyal Order of the Moose is one; the Flat Earth Society is another; the Union of Concerned

Scientists, the Congress of the United States, I could name hundreds more.

Obviously, members of the church can and do belong to many of these organized groups. Yet their participation in God's covenant, their baptism and membership in the church, takes second place to no other commitment. Being part of the people of God is a loyalty that supersedes all others. It follows that whenever the churches become captive to any other human community, whether to nationalism, political entities, social class, or any power but God's, they begin to lose touch with their own identity. The voice of God will be muted, and the purposes for which God has singled out the church will be disrupted.[2]

Part of our problem in seeing the church as that unique community called into existence by God is that it seems so ordinary, so human. We look at the church on Main Street in our town, see its aging buildings, hear its sometimes less-than-splendid sermons, consider its sometimes underwhelming programs, know the foibles of some of its members, and we ask, "Is this the human community God singled out to bear the divine name, proclaim the divine truth, be the vehicle of the divine purpose?" Yes, it is! Step back a couple of paces and see the movement of the church across the generations. With all its humanness and weakness, it has covered the earth with Jesus' name, has indelibly stamped our Western civilization "Christian," has created much of the greatest art, literature, architecture, sculpture, and music the world has ever known, has built hospitals wherever it has gone proclaiming Jesus' name, and has loved the loveless for Jesus' sake. We are the church, *ekklesia,* those called out to bear God's name and purpose in the world.

Set Apart

Carefully read the following verses:

> But you are a chosen race, a royal priesthood, a holy nation, God's own people, that you may declare the wonderful deeds of him who called you out of darkness into his marvelous light. Once you were no people but now you are God's people; once you had not received mercy but now you have received mercy.
>
> —1 Peter 2:9–10

Just about every phrase here lights up the unique purpose for which the church has been called into existence. We are to declare and demonstrate in our actions that God is true and real and loves the world, summoning every son and daughter of Adam to be a son or daughter of Christ. For that purpose we are set apart.

It may sound strange at first, but the idea of being set apart is central to the biblical understanding of holiness. I have an idea that if I were to ask each of you individually, "What is holiness?" you would respond immediately with some comments about good behavior. To be holy is to keep yourself clean from all the dirt out there in the world. Using foul language, drinking too much liquor, engaging in illicit sex, cheating, lying, stealing, carousing—we gotta stay away from all that stuff! That's what we mean by holy, right? Well, not really. Sure, there are passages in the Bible that speak to those issues, but the concept is much broader and richer.

When the Creed says, "I believe in . . . the holy, catholic Church," what does it mean by "holy"? To be holy has only one essential meaning, to be set apart for the purposes of God. The vessels used in temple worship, for instance, plates, bowls, basins, these were holy. Why? Was there some strange property about them? Some divine spirit within them? No, of course not. They were holy only because they were set apart for the service of God. The priests who used the vessels and directed the worship and sacrifice, why were they noly? Not because of their personal merit or moral perfection, but because they had been separated for the service of God. It follows, of course, that those set apart for God's service are to live in God's light.

Why is the church holy? Not because it is perfect pure, or sinless, but because its sin and imperfection lead it to seek the face of God continually, and because it is set apart to bear God's name and purpose in the world. The church is "a holy nation." It is also called "a holy temple" (Eph. 2:21).

One could go a step further and observe that in the Bible nothing is holy in itself but only in relation to God. God alone is holy. Why did the face of Moses shine when he came down from the mountain where he had received the commandments? Why were his eyes aglow, his mouth full of light, and his whole body charged with splendor? Only because he had stood in the glory of God, and it clung to him and irradiated him like the breath of another world.

If the church of Jesus Christ is to be holy, as the New Testament says it is, it will not be for anything that is in us, who are always sinners, but only in that which clings to us because we have been with Jesus. Ultimately, we will accomplish very little unless the love he has given us, the grace he has lavished upon us, and the joy he has planted within us touch the lives of those around us. We are the church, a holy people, because God has chosen to be our God in Jesus Christ and we are set apart to serve God's purposes in the world.

The holiness of the church is never abstract. Holiness is not a property, an accomplishment, or a quality in and of itself. Holiness has no meaning apart from the mission of the church because the church is set apart for a reason, to be the agent of the love of God. We are holy only because the Holy Spirit indwells us and commissions us for service.

Sent Forth

Matthew 28:18–19 is the unforgettable passage we call "the Great Commission." After the resurrection but before the ascension, as his final word, Jesus commissions the church. That is, he gives the church its marching orders:

> All authority in heaven and on earth has been given to me. Go therefore and make disciples of all nations, baptizing them in the name of the Father and of the Son and of the Holy Spirit, teaching them to observe all that I have commanded you; and lo, I am with you always, to the close of the age.

Under this final point I want to deal with the word *catholic*. I guess by now most of us know that when we say "catholic," we use a lowercase *c* and, therefore, do not mean Roman Catholic. *Catholic* is a word brought over into English from the Greek word *katholikos,* meaning "the whole world." When we say that we believe in "the holy, catholic Church," we profess belief in a church that is worldwide in its truth and mission. As Karl Barth observed, "The Church is a *community,* that is, it is an assembly or a place where all who belong to it have a common interest by which they are bound together into a unity."[3]

The unity is not racial, cultural, political, or national.

It does not depend on a common language, a common set of ethnic traditions, or a common cultural perspective; it depends on a common loyalty to Jesus Christ, the Lord of the church. The reason we are one is that we affirm Jesus as the Christ. Whatever hope we have of seeing the face of God in this world and the next is a hope we attach to Jesus, "through [whom] we . . . have access in one Spirit to the Father" (Eph. 2:18).

Some illustrations of this unity may help. Father Varghese was a priest of the Church of South India, studying in the United States. He used to attend worship, listen to some of my sermons, and occasionally take tea at our table. He had long, black whiskers, so long that my small daughter, who watched a lot of cartoons, called him, "Krazy Kat," which he loved. As we talked together about our faith, the differences in our backgrounds would fade away in our common love for Christ.

Sister Talkutnah was an Eskimo woman who still dressed in sealskins and bore the tribal tattoos. She was a member of the Church of the Open Door in Anchorage, Alaska, where I worshiped one summer. When there came a time for open prayer, she would rise and pray in her Eskimo dialect, and one could sense the Spirit of God move across the worshiping assembly. Christ was our common bond.

Thomas Maluit, a slim black man from the southern Sudan, is a Presbyterian minister. He spent time in the church of which I am pastor, walked and talked among us. His grandfather had been killed by a lion, so he knew the dangers of the jungle. That gentle man, who had come from such poverty and had escaped the ravages of civil war, was Christ's man in our midst. Those of us who came to know him felt the bonds of our common faith.

The church is catholic, worldwide in its nature, universal in its appeal, inclusive in its fellowship. One might well quote German theologian Jurgen Moltmann, "It is only when a church is composed of the 'unlike' and the 'different' that it becomes a sign of hope pointing toward the reconciled world of God."[4]

The church is not catholic in the abstract or simply in principle. It is catholic in its calling, and its calling is to bear God's name and fulfill God's purpose in the world. It is catholic as it hears Jesus say, "Make disciples of all nations." We cannot say the church is "holy" unless we also say it is "catholic," for its holiness and catholicity are tied up in its calling to make disciples. Or, to say it another way, the church's nature is inseparable from its mission.

And, as long as I am wound up on this, the church's social witness, its involvement in culture and in the cities of this world, must always be seen through its involvement in the city of God. We possess a dual citizenship and are, therefore, witnesses to that city "whose builder and maker is God" (Heb. 11:10). It is easy to be assimilated into one's culture so thoroughly that the church loses the ability to speak a word from God to its own times, becoming, as comedian Flip Wilson used to say, "The Church of What's Happenin' Now." Some balance is required, sure! The church must know its times, be in touch, conversant, aware, without being assimilated. It must never appear as an antique or a museum piece from another day either! When the church knows itself to be a servant of Christ and knows that it is firmly anchored to human history, to particular times and places, then perhaps it can speak with authority.

"I believe in . . . the holy, catholic church." A church

that is holy and catholic is singled out, set apart, and set forth. Such a church is "a holy nation, God's own people, that [we] may declare the wonderful deeds of him who called [us] out of darkness into his marvelous light."

Questions for Reflection

1. In your experience, when has the church really done what it is called to do?

2. When have you been most disappointed in the church? Why?

3. Consider (discuss) what the chapter says about holiness.

4. Do our churches find their unity in the common confession that Jesus is Lord, as much as in their common social, educational, and economic similarities?

5. Discuss the statement, "The church exists for mission as a fire exists for burning."

11

The Communion of Saints . . .

In terms of this discussion, life begins when the church comprehends the meaning of "the communion of saints." It is a supplementary phrase intended to be taken with the preceding phrase, "I believe in . . . the holy, catholic Church, the communion of saints."

Take a look at the word *saint,* which, I think, has been spoiled by too many paintings of people with halos. A saint is someone who has been canonized into absolute distance from us, a beatific figure with misty, upraised eyes and glowing countenance, hardly human, half-angel. This is *not*—repeat, *not*—what the New Testament means by *saint.* A saint is anyone who professes to be a Christian, someone no better or worse than you. All saints, which is to say "all Christians," are in the process of reconstruction. *Saint* is an English word that comes from the Latin word *sanctus. Sanctus* translates the New Testament word for *holy,* which we learned in the previous chaper does not mean morally perfect, absolutely and unalterably good, good, good! It means, simply and essentially, "set apart." Christians, all of whom are saints, are set apart for the love and service of God, especially as we know God in Jesus Christ. In my parish I address most of my congregational letters, "To all the saints at First Presbyterian." By now most of them have stopped forwarding the letters to the nearest Roman Catholic parish. It is a good Protestant term as well.

The word *communion* requires examination too. The Latin verb *munio* has a primary meaning, "to erect a fortification, to build a wall." The preposition *com* means "together with." Communion, then, is what we do together, a common task or service. It came to mean "company, congregation, assembly," that is, a group of people gathered together to do a particular thing. The communion of saints, then, is what Christians share in common, what they do together, what they are about.

This is a strong word with emotional overtones. To commune with nature is to taste its splendors, to drink in its mystery, to touch its beauty, to feel its power. Nor can you commune unless you open yourself to what nature is, unless you welcome it, call to it, listen to its voice. I remember one blossoming springtime in the woods when I stood before an apple tree, fragrant and in full bloom. So powerful was its beauty, so magnetic its appeal, that all I could think to do was climb up into the branches to immerse myself in its color and fragrance.

In somewhat the same way, it takes openness and self-giving to commune in friendship and love. One must make oneself available, say yes to one's desire to be in relationship, and be ready to both receive and give mutually. To retreat, to contract, to turn inward, to shrink away, is to say no to one's essential need to be in communion with others. Contraction and retreat are the movements of death and not of life; they are, I believe, the cause of many of the illnesses that we bear. We must not hold ourselves so much in reserve!

How much more is the movement of faith a movement of the soul toward God, to be wrapped in God's embrace, a movement of our spirits to seek the breath of God from which they spring.

> Rivers to the ocean run,
> Nor stay in all their course;
> Fire ascending seeks the sun,
> Both speed them to their source.
>
> So my soul, derived from God,
> Longs to view his glorious face,
> Forward tends to his abode
> To rest in his embrace.[1]

The communion of saints is the union of saints with Christ and an undeniable spiritual union with other Christians. Because we are one with him, we are one with one another. That, it seems to me, is a truth essential to any proper understanding of the ecumenical movement.

One other point as we seek to understand the "communion of saints." Since this communion exists within the church, the *ekklesia*, it is a communion that cannot be separated from the calling of the church to be God's people and do God's will. Our communion with Christ and with one another is inseparable from our task of witness and mission. The question, Who are we? cannot stand apart from the question, What are we to do? The holy, catholic church is a communion of saints who are to proclaim the good news of the kingdom of God and of Jesus, the Christ. We are no more than that, and we are no less than that.

The problem is that many people who enter the doors of the sanctuary and sit in the pews are not able to see or experience the church as a communion of saints. Even if we make it easier by calling the church "a community of believers," it doesn't help much. We see the church as a building where certain religious events take place. We see the church as an institution that must maintain property. We see the church as an organization with officers and official boards, pastors and secretaries, committees and financial obligations. But we have a harder time seeing it as a communion of saints.

But isn't that why we exist? Why the investment of our dollars in property and people if not to be what we are and to do what we are called to do? Why expand all this energy just to maintain the outward forms and not to seek the heart of flame that has burned at the center since the day when wind and fire first called the church into being? The buildings, the institution, and the organization exist not for themselves but to tell the Christian story.

Sure it's easier to fiddle with the machinery than to risk the encounter with God. Sure, it's safer to do institutional maintenance than to submit one's life to the searching gaze of Christ. Sure, casual involvements with church life require less than the mutual account-ability so necessary to a community of believers. And it yields a lot less too!

Whether we want to admit it or not, we all need to be part of a mutually acccountable community. Life isn't worth a nickle until we discover groups of people with whom to share life. An amateur baseball team, a club, a volunteer service organization, there are a thousand possibilities. We are social beings and cannot remain in isolation. It follows that the nature of the groups with which we associate, where we make our emotional home deeply affects who we are.

Last year I read Irving Stone's *Origin,* the story of Charles Darwin's life. There is a character named Rowlett, a crew member on one of the long voyages, of whom Darwin says:

Rowlett knew he was dying. He was unwilling to die in England. I never heard him mention having a home there or family or friends. He was out on the first *Adventure* for five years, and now two and a half years with us. The *Beagle* was his home, and we his family. That's why he wanted to die on board.[2]

What are the communities to which you belong? Why? What do they contribute to your life? Where do you feel "at home"? Is it not true that we are really alive when we are with other people—whether for leisure, for service, or for faith—with them in such a way that the walls between us crumble a little and we feel a communion together?

I've observed some things about the nature of the Christian community. It is not, and I have said it more than once, a perfect community. Those of you who are perfect will be disappointed. Did you ever hear these lines?

> To live in love with the saints above,
>   O that will be glory!
> But to live below with the saints I know,
>   That's another story!

The first characteristic of the Christian community I want to mention is that, *it is an accepting and forgiving community*. That's the way it is in a family. Sure, there are problems. Sure, we sometimes hurt and disappoint one another. Sure, we fail to love as we should. But we are bound together by ties of mutual commitment, by blood, and by years spent in relationship, and we keep working at it. There are good times, celebrations, laughter, mutual discovery, and times when we are able to say, "I love you." The things that hold us together are stronger than the things that would separate us. And while there are many broken families, while our own imperfections drive us apart, we can see how much we need one another, even in the midst of our pain. It means everthing to know that there is a family, or a group of people who serve as family, who cares for us, accepts us for what we are, forgives our frailties, and holds us accountable for our actions. I don't know about you, but I hope the church can be that kind of community. Indeed, for many of us, it is.

There is a second characteristic of the Christian community I want to mention: *It is a community committed to mutual discovery*. What does that mean? It means not being static, sterile, or stuck. It means pushing out the walls so that our lives are wider. It means personal adventure into the unknown. It means facing our dark places so that light can penetrate, illuminate, motivate. If I cannot see myself further down the road this year in knowing, in loving, in really being alive, then what's the use?

That means worship. But just as important, it means the ways we are together elsewhere in the church. Along with the work that must be done to keep the institution healthy, a true vehicle for the gospel, we must find places to ask our essential questions: What does it mean to be a Christian today? What keeps me from believing? What can I affirm? What troubles me most? What do I fear or hope for with all my heart? Where am I going? What is my own experience of the love of Christ? Many of us find it hard to ask these questions. Yet if we fail to ask them, how can we be the church? It is at the point where we face up to our great struggles, our doubt and pain, that the gospel comes to life. It is then that Christ steps out of obscurity and meets us in the middle of our life's journey. The church must be a community of mutual discovery.

There is a third and final characteristic of the church that I want to mention: *It is the community of the Spirit.* One Pentecost we hung a thirty-foot red-and-white banner from our carillon tower. Someone at a nearby restaurant asked if it were a picture of a satellite. I smiled and said, "No, it is a descending dove, symbol of the descent of the Spirit that brought the Christian church to birth." I didn't go on to say that a resurrected Jesus had told disciples to remain in Jerusalem until they were "clothed with power from on high" (Luke 24:49), and that there had been a strange descent of fire and a whistling wind that filled that group of Jesus' people with a new energy to tell Jesus' story. They had gathered, they had joined their human spirits in expectant waiting, one united, heartfelt longing for Christ. One can never capture what happened in words. In symbol of flame, which is transforming energy, and in symbol of wind, which is motivating force and elemental breath of God, the Spirit came and the church was born. Whatever else it may be, however else it may be described, the church is the community of the Spirit. It is more than us, our human ingenuity, our pooled moral resources, our plans and strategies. When the church is at its best, then, as Paul said, "It is the Spirit . . . bearing witness with our spirit that we are children of God" (Rom. 8:16). As we become part of the communion of saints, the clarity and power of this Spirit will seal the truth in our hearts, like an inextinguishable light, so that we know a risen Christ, alive through the power of God's Spirit, present for God's people.

In that wild and wonderful passage in Hebrews, sometimes called "the catalogue of the heroes and heroines of the faith," all that they suffered and accomplished, there appears that rather astonishing statement, "since we are surrounded by so great a cloud of witnesses" (12:1). The image is that of the Olympic Games, of a stadium full of spectators, of the athletes on the racecourse being cheered on. It is another way of picturing the communion of saints. All those believers who have left this life, who are now united with God, are still the church. They also belong to the assembly of the faithful. They participate with us in ways we cannot comprehend. They are one with us in the love and service of God, forming an integral part of the communion of saints.

> O blest communion, fellowship divine!
> We feebly struggle, they in glory shine;
> Yet all are one within your great design.
> Alleluia! Alleluia![3]

Because we are the community of the Spirit, we are the church. Because we are the church, we belong to Christ and are one with him. Because we are one with him, we make his love visible in the world.

Questions for Reflection

1. "Keep you troubles to yourself!" Compare and/or contrast this to the "communion of saints."

2. Why are some people more "at home" in a secular service organization than they are in the church?

3. Do you agree that "who we are cannot be separated from what we do"? That identity determines action?

4. Recall a time when you experienced the communion of saints.

— 12 —

The Forgiveness of Sins . . .

The Apostles' Creed, structured in three major sections, affirms the trinitarian belief of the early church, a belief that God is revealed to us in three persons: Father, Son, and Holy Spirit. This self-revelation is God's way of being God, manifestations given to us of God's nature and purposes. This chapter is the third subject in the third section on the Holy Spirit. Every Sunday it is part of the liturgy of worship in just about every Christian church, "the forgiveness of sins." Here are three key words to carry us through the chapter: *explanation, experience, expression.*

Explanation

Even as I list this first point, I am struck by the thought that many Christian writers and most Christian preachers suffer from a compulsion to explain everything. If we can reduce it to a neat definition, if we can describe it in a few deft phrases, if we can characterize it, categorize it, catalog it, then we will have captured it, right? No, wrong! Many of the deeper realities of the Christian faith can never be "captured." We have to take off our shoes, we have to bring heart, emotions, inner hungers, and intuition, or the truth remains elusive. This is certainly true of the forgiveness of sins. Sometimes there is a paralysis in too much analysis. When we have finished our explanations, we remain strangers to the thing we have taken pains to explain. We remain observers but not participants.

I was amused when I read this sentence by Karl Barth. I'm sure he must have smiled when he wrote it, "It is always a danger and a seduction to write such thick volumes of dogmatics."[1] He, of course, wrote prodigious volumes of dogmatic theology—but he knew they were only words on paper unless people brought more than their minds to Christian faith.

Here is an illustration I have chosen from Dostoevsky's *Crime and Punishment* to demonstrate that explanations are never sufficient to satisfy our human condition. Forgiveness, for instance, is encountered not merely in the mind but in the bones and in the blood, in the hope and fear and failure of life. A young student named Raskolnikov commits a terrible crime. He murders two people for their money. Then he tries to rationalize the crime. Napoleon, he tells himself, murdered thousands and became a hero. The two he murdered were only miserly, insignificant people, and he would use the money to advance his career for the good of humankind. But the rationalization doesn't work, and the crime grinds away at his life from the inside.

A young woman named Sonya loves Raskolnikov, and her love prompts him to confess to her what he has done. When she learns of this, she tells him that he must go to the center of town where the murders were committed, and there, on his knees, he must kiss the earth which has been defiled with the blood of two innocent human beings. Then he is to rise and cry out to the north, east, south, and west that he is a murderer. It is her love that compels him, tortured as he is, to consider the confession. In the power of her love he sees the true nature of what he has done and who he is, and as a result, he cries out to the whole world the nature of his transgression.

He is arrested, convicted, and sent off to Siberia for eight years. Sonya goes with him, all the long miles, and she keeps the two of them alive by foraging for potatoes and cabbages, almost dying herself. The point is that her love is more than an explanation or a theory; it is a passionate giving of the self and has such power that Raskolnikov is able to see who he is and make his powerful, life-changing confession.

In the great final scene, the crime confessed, the punishment borne in the strength of the love so freely given, he knows forgiveness and experiences a resurrection to new life. The peace of God is his.

Perhaps a brief explanation will be helpful. The basic New Testament word for "forgiveness" means "to release, to let go, to liberate." Forgiveness is seen as a loosing of the chains that bind us, a freeing from the confinement of a life lived out of harmony with God and neighbor. Perhaps you will recall the passage in *Pilgrim's Progress* in which Christian has been laboring along the road that leads to the Celestial City. Strapped to his back is a huge load he has been carrying, a load that wearies him, burdens him, weighs him down. It is the crushing weight of his sins. Finally, after his long struggle, he comes to the foot of the cross of Jesus Christ, and he kneels there. Immediately, "his burden loosed from off his shoulders, and fell off his back, and began to tumble, and so continued to do until it came to the mouth of the sepulchre, where it fell in, and was seen no more." Forgiveness, made possible through the sacrificial love of Jesus, releases us from the burden of our sins. If it will help, we can call that burden, "guilt," or "emptiness," or "brokenness."

Experience

For years Tom Anderson's life was blighted by a bitter memory. He had participated in a hazing ceremony in college that resulted in the death of a fellow student. He floundered from one job to another. He and his wife separated after six years of marriage. Then the news about Tom changed. He and his wife got back together; he earned a fine position in the business world. This was his explanation for the change:

> I used to think, "Nothing can undo what I have done." The thought of my guilt would stop me in the middle of a smile or a handshake. It put a wall between Betty and me. Then I had an unexpected visit from the person I most dreaded to see—the mother of the college classmate who died.
>
> "Years ago," she said, "I found it in my heart, through prayer, to forgive you. Betty forgave you. So did your friends and employers." She paused, and then said sternly, "You are the only person who hasn't forgiven Tom Anderson. Who do you think you are to stand out against the people of the town and the Lord Almighty?"
>
> I looked into her eyes and found there a kind of permission to be the person I might have been if her boy had lived. For the first time in my adult life I felt worthy to love and be loved.[2]

Tom Anderson had no trouble experiencing his guilt. Indeed, it was ruining his life. Maybe it is not so easy for some of the rest of us to feel, to accept our own need for forgiveness. We haven't killed anybody or robbed any banks. We make our way through the morning confession of sin during worship without a lot of involvement. A sinner? Who, us?

Yet who of us is not ready to admit that there is a tragic flaw at the very heart and center of human experience? Look at our history written in blood across the centuries—war, greed, betrayal, selfishness, hatred—we are not strangers to these things. And not just humankind as a whole but each of us as individuals. There are tendencies within me that frighten me, pools of darkness I can neither understand nor explain. Good things, yes, many of them, but a kind of disharmony, as if something within me were at war with my own essence, my own being. No wonder Paul wrote, "The good that I would I do not: but the evil which I would not, that I do. . . . O wretched man that I am! who shall deliver me?" (Rom. 7:19,24, KJV).

The experience of the inner state of our own unrest can take the shape of guilt, self-hatred, or poor self-image. It is a sign that the self is out of harmony with its own essence and, therefore, with God. Or it can take the shape of grudge, those little hurts we store away in our hearts, around which we are tempted to nurse our grievances, build our resentment, and plan our revenge. This behavior is corrosive and will hide the face of God.

Guilt, grudge, and resentment are all contractions of the inner life. They are the human spirit drawing in upon itself. They represent narrowing, constriction, and confinement and are, as I have observed before, the movements of death. Perhaps that is why James said, "Sin when it is full-grown brings forth death" (1:15).

On the other hand, confession, repentance, forgiveness, and love are all expansive. They are a kind of palms-up, arms-extended receptivity, the soul moving out from itself seeking God and others. They represent widening horizons, personal growth, self-giving, which are the movements of life. Perhaps that is why Paul said, "The law of the Spirit of life in Christ Jesus has set me free from the law of sin and death" (Rom. 8:2).

One could hardly write about the forgiveness of sins within a Christian framework without dwelling on the death of Jesus as the experience above all others from which our forgiveness flows. When we talk about forgiveness as Christianity knows it, we are not giving a philosophical disquisition, we are not presenting an illuminating instruction about the idea of God; rather we are bearing witness to God's action in Jesus Christ. It is this deed, this gift, that calls the sinner to repentance and faith and constitutes the church as the people of God. It is not really a question of ethical living, good conduct, or religious propriety—none of these things yield forgiveness and new life. It is a Christ who gazed down at those who wielded the hammer, plaited the thorns into a crown, and lifted him up between heaven and earth—a Christ who saw all this and prayed, "Father, forgive them; for they know not what they do" (Luke 23:34).

This kind of self-giving love, forgiving love, demonstrates *to us* how God feels *about us*. It is a love unqualified, unfettered, unreserved, that sees us as we are and loves us still. Hear the astonishment of the New Testament writer, "While we were yet sinners Christ died for us" (Rom. 5:8). If we are ever to move within the doors of the kingdom of God, it will be because we see at last that Jesus does this for us, in obedience to the will of the Father.

Just as the death of Christ is pivotal for understanding

the nature of the New Testament, so forgiveness is the theme of themes which is sounded and the song of songs which is sung. Karl Barth observed, "The forgiveness of sins is the basis, the sum, the criterion, of all that may be called Christian life or faith."[3]

Forgiveness is the foundation upon which the whole structure of Christianity rests. It is bedrock. We are accepted by God! God has an irresistible prejudice in our favor. Our acceptance of God's acceptance of us, our inner experience of acceptance, was one of the great keys to faith that appeared so often in the writing of Paul Tillich, as in this sermon:

> One of the great and liberating experiences of the Protestant reformers was their realization that our relation to God is not dependent on the continuous repetition of words of prayer and thanks directed to God, on sacrifices and other rituals, but rather on the serenity and joy that is the answer to the good news that we are accepted by God.[4]

Will we speak of Christianity and the arts, Christianity and culture, Christianity and social problems, Christianity and the individual? We will do so, and our approach will be colored and inevitably shaped by the forgiveness of sins.

A parish near Worcester, England, is known as "Upton Snodsbury with Beauchamp, and Grafton Flyford with North Piddle and Flyford Favell." One wonders how secretaries answer the phone. But more important, what is the feeling tone of parish life? After we have talked about answering the phone, mowing the grass, and keeping the books, what bubbles up just beneath the surface? What is the consciousness that permeates and lifts a congregation's life? It must be, and can be, the forgiveness of sins. Our falseness, our persistent darkness, our failures in living and loving are forgiven, and we are accepted and given grace to change and grow through nothing else than the self-giving of our Lord Jesus Christ.

Expression

Jesus told a story about a servant on a large estate who owed the master of the estate a debt of many thousands of dollars. When he could not pay, the master freely forgave him the whole sum. Later that day, this forgiven servant faced a fellow servant who owed him a few dollars, and when the debtor could not pay, he had him thrown into prison. The master of the estate, when he heard this, was very angry and said, in effect, "You have been forgiven so much. Could you not have forgiven so little?" And the master delivered him to the jailers till he could pay all he had owed. Jesus ended with the stern words, "So also my heavenly Father will do to every one of you, if you do not forgive your brother from your heart" (Matt. 18:35).

The teaching is simple and direct: We who stand under the forgiving love of God, which we do not deserve and could never earn, are we not to forgive others? Can we not find it within ourselves, since we bear Christ's name, to live out a life of forgiving love, standing in the shoes of the other person?

In 1955 there was a move by Japanese statesmen to restore Japan's image in the Philippine Islands, which they had desolated. A mission was sent from Tokyo to Manila at a moment when bitterness between the two nations had intensified—negotiations about Japanese reparations had collapsed after years of deadlock. When Niro Hoshijima, a senior member of the Japanese Diet, rose to address a packed Manila theater, he was shouted down. Finally, gaining a hearing, he said:

> "My government has asked me to tell you that Japan must and will pay reparations—in full. But reparations—are not enough. First of all, we must sincerely apologize for the past and humbly ask your forgiveness." Struck dumb by this admission, the Filipino audience listened in silence as Hoshijima begged the nation for forgiveness; then there was thunderous applause. Afterward, many Filipinos pressed forward to shake the speaker's hand. Some wept. Said one, "These wrists of mine will always bear the mark of Japanese handcuffs, but tonight I have forgiven you."

Reparation agreements were reached one year later.[5]

If only we had the courage to admit it when we are wrong, to say, "I am sorry." If only we had the grace to forgive those who have committed wrongs against us.

Listen! Those of you who are letting misunderstandings run on from year to year, meaning to clear them up someday; you who are keeping wretched quarrels alive because you cannot bring yourself to sacrifice your pride and kill them; you who are letting someone's heart starve for a word of appreciation, which you mean to give someday; if only you could see how short the time is, how your word or action could break the evil spell, you would go and do it. You would express forgiveness because it is the human thing to do, the loving thing to do, and because God in Christ has forgiven you. The one (or ones) you forgave would feel, perhaps, what Jacob felt when he was forgiven by his brother Esau, "I have seen thy face, as though I had seen the face of God" (Gen. 33:10 KJV).

What power and meaning in this phrase from the Creed, "I believe in . . . the forgiveness of sins"!

Questions for Reflection

1. What experience of being forgiven do you remember? Of forgiving?

2. Why is forgiveness central for Christians?

3. How can the church discover the power of forgiveness in its life and worship?

4. How does "the forgiveness of sins" affect our relationships with, or our attitudes toward people regarded as social outcasts? Who are they?

5. Have I learned to forgive myself for wrongs long remembered, as God has forgiven me in Christ?

13

The Resurrection of the Body, and the Life Everlasting . . .

This chapter is the final installment of our learn-as-you-go plan for studying, grappling with, and absorbing the truth and beauty of the Apostles' Creed. I have been saying that there are three sections in the Creed—God the Father Almighty, Jesus Christ his only Son our Lord, and the Holy Spirit—corresponding, of course, to our trinitarian belief that God is made known to us in three distinct but inseparable persons. The present chapter considers the last article of belief in the last section of the Creed, an article that affirms the reality of "the resurrection of the body, and the life everlasting."

In discussing this wonderful teaching of the Christian faith, I will base most of my remarks on First Corinthians 15, the resurrection chapter of the New Testament. Here we are looking at the earliest written evidence for Jesus' rising from the dead. At this time in the first century there were no written Gospels, since the first letter to Corinth was written about twenty years after the crucifixion. Many who had known Jesus would still be living, and Paul listed some of them by name, people who saw Jesus alive again after his public execution. One is struck by the more than five hundred Christians who saw Jesus on a single occasion, "most of whom," said Paul, "are still alive" (1 Cor. 15:6). He made no attempt to persuade his readers or to prove the resurrection. There is no artistic embellishment. He said, in effect, "These are the historic facts as we know them."[1]

As we consider this last section of the Creed, three words can serve as signposts to mark our way: the *pattern,* the *promise,* and the *prospect.*

The Pattern

The pattern is simply this: Christ's resurrection becomes the guarantee of our own. In First Corinthians 15:22 we read, "As in Adam all die, so also in Christ shall all be made alive." I wonder if this essential truth of Christianity has ever become clear to us? Where does our hope of forgiveness lie? In the death of Christ. Where does our hope of eternal life lie? In the resurrection of Christ. We identify ourselves with him. We yield ourselves to him—his love, his knowledge of God, his power, his person, his ultimate values, his very self. That is why we call him "Lord," because we submit our lives to his authority, to who and what he is as Son of God and Savior. That is why we pray, "Lord Jesus, come into my heart."

> Jesus, Thy blood and righteousness
> My beauty are, my glorious dress;
> 'Midst flaming worlds in these arrayed,
> With joy shall I lift up my head.[2]

This reality of Jesus is central to the gospel not peripheral. This is not one way to look at it; this is not the theology of a few enthusiasts; this is Christianity. To be a Christian is to be a woman or a man in Christ and to have received the resurrection message. On this subject Hans Küng remarks, "This is common to all New Testament writing without exception."[3]

If ever I am to come to a firm Christian faith, if ever I am to feel myself included in the community of Christian believers, I will first need to place myself, irrevocably, in the care and keeping of Jesus Christ. If you want a central text for this, try this one: "I am crucified with Christ: nevertheless I live; yet not I, but Christ liveth in me: and the life which I now live in the flesh I live by the faith of the Son of God, who loved me, and gave himself for me" (Gal. 2:20, KJV).

The patterning event for "the resurrection of the body, and the life everlasting," which is affirmed in the Creed, is the resurrection of Christ. As First Corinthians attests, this is the cornerstone event for Christianity. Upon it the whole structure of our faith rests. Paul said, "If Christ has not been raised, your faith is futile" (1 Cor. 15:17). Every time we talk of a living Christ, every time we invoke his presence in our midst, every time we break bread and pour wine, every time we confess, "Jesus Christ is Lord," we acknowledge and celebrate the resurrection. Without it Christianity would never have survived the first century of its existence, never have survived, in fact, the crucifixion.

The resurrection, moreover, is an event firmly anchored in history. If we did not know it through the New Testament, we would have to hypothesize it to explain the things that followed—the birth of the church, its explosive rise and prominence despite intense persecution, its permeation of the Roman Empire, its staying power, its innate and inherent force. No wonder the church proclaims across the generations, "The Lord is risen," and the hearts of the faithful respond, "He is risen indeed!"

Madeleine L'Engle likes First Corinthians 15. She says, "I stand with Paul here. When we deny the Resurrection, we are denying Christianity."[4] The pattern is simple, "Because he lives, we too shall live."

The Promise

The promise is "the resurrection of the body." "Well," you say, "that's pretty far out. What does that mean?" Let me give you a couple of quotes for starters and then expand the meaning of the promise. German theologian Jurgen Moltmann says, "Anyone who says 'God' and does not hope for the resurrection of the dead and a new creation from the righteousness of God has not said 'God.'"[5] Hans Küng says, "Anyone who seriously believes in the living God believes therefore also in the raising of the dead to life."[6]

Most of us, hearing quotes like these, will say, "Well, of course! Everybody knows that Christians believe in life to come!" Yet there is a way of thinking that has made its way into the minds of many church people. It sounds like this, "When you're dead, you're dead!" Or "Better live right now, it's the only chance you've got!"

Christianity without the horizon of the resurrection is like the sky without stars, life without love, or springtime without flowers. We just can't imagine one without the other. Christianity would become merely sociology or, at best, practical ethics.

Clearly, then, we must be against any point of view that, for whatever reason, denies the resurrection and eternal life. The resurrection of Christ and of the Christian believer is the horizon without which our faith loses its essential meaning.

For if there were no Easter, there'd be no Christmas. If the child had grown up and died . . . period, who today would remember the magic night of his birth? For no Resurrection story, then no New Testament, no church, no Christianity.[7]

Notice that Christianity does not argue the resurrection from human reason. Yes, there is an upward movement from the dust toward the stars. Yes, life develops from the simple to the complex, from inanimate matter to immaterial spirit. Yes, nature knows not extinction but only transformation. Yes, evolution is not merely the adaptation of forms to their environment and the survival of the fittest but rather creativity and the transcendence of life forms beyond their present state. Nevertheless, as fascinating as these things may be, and as much truth as they may carry, Christianity places its only hope of life to come in the person of Jesus Christ and in the event of his resurrection. John gave this statement as the reason he wrote his Gospel: "These [things] are written that you may believe that Jesus is the Christ, the Son of God, and that believing you may have life in his name" (20:31).

It was not the empty tomb that convinced the early disciples, nor the graveclothes left collapsed and empty, nor the stone rolled back from the sepulcher. It was their experience of a living Christ. So it has been for the church in every generation. So it will be for us. Across the centuries he speaks still, "I am the resurrection and the life; he who believes in me, though he die, yet shall he live, and whoever lives and believes in me shall never die" (John 11:25–26). This is the promise. It has Easter as its guarantee.

The Prospect

The prospect is "the life everlasting."

Sometimes, when I am working in my garden, when the day is hot and still, I am transported to another world. The hum of bees seems like singing wires from Eternity. It is as though a message were trying to come through and I know what it means but I can't hear the words . . . I like to think my garden is Eden, but I know it is only *evidence* of Eden.

No, that isn't Ron James in his backyard; that is Dorothy Gardner in *Eastward in Eden* (Act 1).

The hope of life to come is so persistent in the human race that we suppress it only with great difficulty. We may give it as our opinion that we do not believe in a future life, but in our native impulses we believe. The Great Pyramids of Giza and the golden treasures of Tutankhamen are mute but eloquent testimony to this ineradicable human hope. Saint Augustine was right in saying to God, "Thou madest us for Thyself, and our heart is restless, until it repose in Thee."

Though you and I may wonder about this a great deal, the Bible does not talk much about the geography and furniture of heaven. Jesus mentioned a house with many rooms and said, "I go to prepare a place for you" (John 14:2). But one searches in vain for details. Here and there the New Testament contains a fascinatingly vague line:

Things beyond our seeing, things beyond our hearing, things beyond our imagining, all prepared by God for those who love him.

—1 Corinthians 2:9, NEB

134

Lo! I tell you a mystery. We shall not all sleep, but we shall all be changed, in a moment, in the twinkling of an eye, at the last trumpet. For the trumpet will sound, and the dead will be raised imperishable, and we shall be changed.

—1 Corinthians 15:51–52

Beloved, we are God's children now; it does not yet appear what we shall be.

—First John 3:2

It is obvious in the Gospel accounts that some things about Jesus were the same and some things were different. The disciples recognized him, but only when he spoke. Early on Easter morning at the tomb, Mary recognized him, but only when he called her name. He was the same, but he was different. The disciples on the Emmaus Road did not recognize him until he broke bread and prayed at their table. How strange! His body took a recognizable form that was somehow dissimilar until personal contact was made.

When one reads through the Gospel accounts of his postresurrection appearances, time and distance seem inconsequential. He is in Galilee, then he is in Jerusalem, ninety miles to the south. The disciples are in a room with locked doors, but he suddenly appears in their midst and is gone just as suddenly. He makes a fire on the shore of the Lake of Galilee and cooks a breakfast of fish. Always he says, "Do not be afraid" and "I am with you."

Clearly, there has been a transformation of life, a metamorphosis, some sort of existence within a new dimension. There is a body, but one with mysterious and wondrous powers, a body perhaps not fettered with the limitations of time, space, and materiality. Is this the resurrection body of First Corinthians 15, a body capable of living without limits in God's limitless future? Well, who knows? It would seem that it is a real body but one with new properties and new possibilities. After all, that new life to come, that "life everlasting," is not totally different from the life we live here and now. There is only one Reality over which God rules. It is the same life transposed into a higher, more profound harmony.

What we see in a resurrected Christ is eternal life within time. It is a prospect of things to come, We, like Christ, shall have a resurrection body capable of fulfilling the eternal purposes for which God created us. Each of us shall become what God intends, each reach and realize full potential. This life is prologue, then the drama will begin. We can never use that as an excuse to avoid living fully in this world, but we can look wonderingly on that eternal horizon. Yes, we accept our humanity, for we are children of the dust. We treasure the years that are given to us, even with their pain. We smell the flowers as we pass by. And, because we are Christians, we love neighbors gladly for Jesus' sake. But all the while, though we may love life dearly and know the warmth of being at home here, still we know there is an eternal city whose builder and maker is God. Every day brings us closer to that homeland.

What a way to end the Apostles' Creed, on this note of triumph! There will be a day when "the kingdom of the world has become the kingdom of our Lord and of his Christ, and he shall reign for ever and ever" (Rev. 11:15).

So, we are at an end. And in the light of what has been discussed, where are you? Having come this far, having pondered, questioned, struggled, perhaps having seen some new dimensions of the faith or having had the walls of mind and heart pushed out a bit, where are you? How can I end without an appeal to faith in Jesus Christ, on whom the Creed centers from beginning to end? Do you trust him? Are you "in Christ"? Have you rested your restless heart in him? Can you say with the Creed, "I believe?" If not, why not? Go at least as far as the father who begged Jesus to heal his son, "I believe; help my unbelief" (Mark 9:24).

Questions for Reflection

1. In what ways does the church teach our identification with Christ? Sacraments? Small group life? Worship? Congregational mood or consciousness?

2. Do you believe in life after death? Why? Why not?

3. What does the Bible mean by heaven? Will we know who we are? Will we recognize those we love?

4. Discuss Jesus' promise, "Because I live, you too shall live" (John 14:19). Quote similar verses.

5. Are Christians afraid of death? Why? Why not?

Notes

Chapter 1
1. Hippolytus, *Apostolic Tradition* (question 21).

Chapter 2
1. *Catechism of the Church of Geneva* (questions 21–22).
2. Karl Barth, *The Faith of the Church* (New York: Fontana Books, 1960), p. 34.
3. *Heidelberg Catechism* (question 26).
4. Hymn, "God Moves in a Mysterious Way." William Cowper
5. Ibid.
6. Barth, *Faith of the Church,* pp. 38–39.
7. Fritjof Capra, *The Turning Point* (New York: Simon & Schuster, 1982), p. 78.
8. Ibid., p. 86.

Chapter 3
1. Albert Camus, *Resistance, Rebellion, and Death* (New York: Vintage Books, 1974), p. 9.
2. C. S. Lewis, *Miracles* (New York: Macmillan, 1947), pp. 96–97, 114.
3. Harry Emerson Fosdick, *The Man from Nazareth* (New York: Pocket Books, 1953), p. 141.
4. Hans Küng, *On Being a Christian* (Garden City, N. Y.: Doubleday, 1976), p. 448.
5. Barth, *Faith of the Church,* p. 61.
6. Ernest Campbell, "Questions Jesus Asked: Who do you say that I

am?" (Sermon preached at the Riverside Church, New York City, April 4, 1976.)

7. Tom Driver, *Patterns of Grace* (New York: Harper & Row, 1977), p. 149.
8. *Catechism of the Church of Geneva* (question 48).
9. *Heidelberg Catechism* (question 34).
10. Edward Danks, "Jesus Christ Is Lord," (Sermon preached at the Noroton Presbyterian Church, Darien, Connecticut, September 24, 1978.)

Chapter 4
1. Barth, *Faith of the Church*, pp. 68–69.
2. William Barclay, *The Gospel of John*, vol. 1 (Philadelphia: Westminster Press, 1955), p. 46.
3. E. Stanley Jones, *The Word Became Flesh* (Nashville: Abingdon Press, 1963), p. 7.
4. Madeleine L'Engle, *The Irrational Season* (Minneapolis: Seabury Press, 1979), p. 27.
5. *Ibid*, p. 111.

Chapter 5
1. Sheldon Vanauken, *A Severe Mercy* (New York: Harper & Row, 1977), p. 99.
2. Elie Wiesel, *Night*. Quoted in *The Crucified God* by Jurgen Moltmann (New York: Harper and Row, 1974), pp. 273–274.

Chapter 7
1. From a sermon preached at the Community Church, San Marino, California, June 22, 1980, by the Reverend Patrick Thyne.
2. A. E. Taylor, *The Faith of a Moralist*, series 2 (New York: Kraus Reprint Co., 1969), p. 141.
3. Leslie Weatherhead, *The Transforming Friendship* (Dumfries, Va.: Wyvern Books, 1962), p. 36.

Chapter 8
1. *The New York Times*, February 4, 1976, section C, p. 29.
2. Charles Krauthammer, "The End of the World," *The New Republic*, March 28, 1983, pp. 12–13.
3. Ibid., p. 12.
4. Ibid.
5. *Hamlet*, act 5, sc. 2, line 10.
6. Hymn, "God Is Working His Purpose Out," in *The Worshipbook* (Philadelphia: Westminster Press, 1970).
7. Ibid. (from Isa. 11:9).
8. *Heidelberg Catchism* (question 52).

Chapter 9
1. Hymn, "Come Thou Almighty King," in *The Methodist Hymnal* (Nashville: Methodist Publishing House).
2. Karl Barth, *Credo* (New York: Scribners, 1962), p. 128.
3. Hugh Thompson Kerr, ed., *A Compend of Luther's Theology* (Philadelphia: Westminster Press, 1943), p. 65.

Chapter 10
1. F L. Cross and E. A. Livingstone, eds., *The Oxford Dictionary of the Christian Church* (Oxford: Oxford University Press, 1974), p. 75.
2. Barth, *Credo,* p. 138.
3. Ibid., p. 137.
4. Jurgen Moltmann, "God Reconciles and Makes Free," in *A Study Book for Delegates, World Alliance of Reformed Churches* August 1970, p. 8.

Chapter 11
1. Hymn, "Rise, My Soul," in *The Hymnal* (Presbyterian Board of Christian Education, 1933).
2. Irving Stone, *The Origin* (Garden City, N.Y.: Doubleday, 1980), p. 283.
3. Hymn, "For All the Saints," in *The Worshipbook* (Philadelphia: Westminster Press, 1972).

Chapter 12
1. Barth, *Faith of the Church,* p. 134.
2. *Reader's Digest,* March 1961, p. 43.
3. Barth, *Faith of the Church,* p. 133.
4. Paul Tillich, *The Eternal Now* (New York: Scribners, 1963), pp. 178–79.
5. *Reader's Digest,* January 1968, p. 152.

Chapter 13
1. J. B. Phillips, *Ring of Truth* (New York: Macmillan, 1967), p. 32.
2. Hymn, "Jesus Thy Blood and Righteousness," in *Hymns for the Family of God* (Nashville: Paragon).
3. Küng, *On Being a Christian,* p. 347.
4. L'Engle, *Irrational Season,* p. 93.
5. Jurgen Moltmann, *The Crucified God* (New York: Harper & Row, 1974), p. 218.
6. Küng, *On Being a Christian,* p. 361.
7. Edmund A. Steimle, *God the Stranger* (Philadelphia: Fortress Press, 1979), p. 6.

Ron James is Senior Pastor at the First Presbyterian Church of Stamford, Connecticut. He received a Master of Divinity degree from Fuller Theological Seminary in Pasadena, California and Master of Arts degree from Harvard University in Cambridge, Massachusetts.

Mr. James enjoys trout fishing, canoeing, and folk guitar. He and his wife Lois have four children, Steven, Kristin, Jennifer, and David.